Members of the FDIC Unbanked/Underbanked Survey Study Group
Authors:
Susan Burhouse, Karyen Chu, Ryan Goodstein, Joyce Northwood, Yazmin Osaki, Dhruv Sharma
Contributors:
Keith Ernst, Alicia Lloro, Sherrie Rhine

Table of Contents

1. Executive Summary and Implications..4

2. Background and Objectives 13

3. Banking Status of U.S. Households 15

4. Checking and Savings Account Ownership, and Automatic Transfers.....................28

5. Prepaid Debit Cards...29

6. Alternative Financial Services 41

7. Access to Mobile Phones and the Internet 50

8. Banking Methods 53

9. Implications and Conclusion..62

Appendix A — K...Published Separately

1. Executive Summary and Implications

When households open an account at a federally insured depository institution, they establish a mainstream banking relationship. This relationship provides opportunities for households to deposit funds securely, conduct basic financial transactions, accumulate savings, and access credit on fair and affordable terms.

Despite these benefits, many households—referred to in this report as "unbanked"—do not have an account at an insured institution. Additional households have an account, but have also obtained financial services and products from non-bank, alternative financial services (AFS) providers in the prior 12 months. These households are referred to here as "underbanked." The existence of unbanked and underbanked households presents an opportunity for banks to expand access to their products and services and forge relationships with these underserved groups, ultimately increasing economic inclusion.

The FDIC recognizes that public confidence in the banking system is strengthened when banks effectively serve the broadest possible set of consumers. As a result, the agency is committed to increasing the participation of unbanked and underbanked households in the financial mainstream. The FDIC National Survey of Unbanked and Underbanked Households represents one contribution to this end.

Conducted to assess the inclusiveness of the banking system, and in partial response to a statutory mandate, the biennial survey provides estimates of unbanked and underbanked populations. It also seeks to provide insights that will inform efforts to better meet the needs of these consumers. The FDIC partnered with the U.S. Census Bureau to administer this survey in June 2013, collecting responses from 40,998 households.

Key Findings

Banking Status of U.S. Households

One in thirteen households was unbanked in 2013. This proportion decreased from 2011, reflecting changed economic conditions and household demographics. An additional one in five households was underbanked in 2013.

- 7.7 percent of households in the United States were unbanked in 2013. This proportion repre-

sented nearly 9.6 million households composed of approximately 16.7 million adults and 8.7 million children.[1]

- 20.0 percent (24.8 million) of U.S. households were underbanked in 2013, meaning that they had a bank account but also used alternative financial services (AFS) outside of the banking system.[2] Approximately 50.9 million adults and 16.6 million children lived in underbanked households.

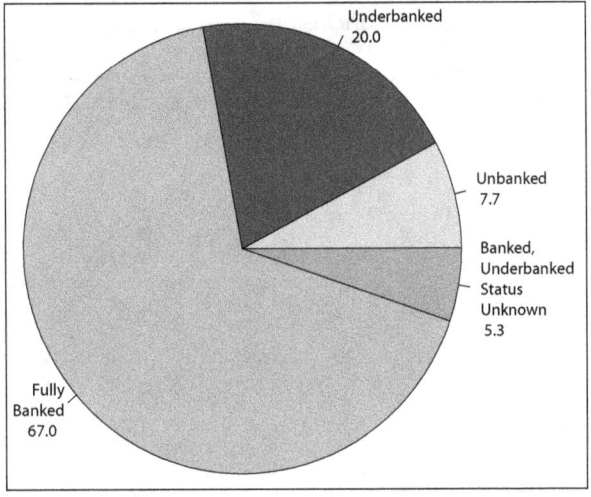

Figure ES.1 Banking Status Of U.S. Households, 2013

- The unbanked rate has varied from 7.6 percent in 2009 to 8.2 percent in 2011 and 7.7 percent in 2013.[3]

  - The 0.5 percentage point decrease in the unbanked rate between 2011 and 2013 can be explained by differences in the economic

---

[1] Adults are defined as people aged 16 and older. This is a lower-bound estimate of the number of unbanked adults in the United States because it is based on the assumption that all adults residing in a "banked" household are banked in the sense that they may benefit from the account. A banked household may have one or more unbanked adults; these unbanked adults residing in banked households are not included in the 16.7 million adults figure cited in this report.

[2] In the 2013 survey, underbanked households are those that have used at least one of the following AFS from non-bank providers in the last 12 months: money orders, check cashing, remittances, payday loans, refund anticipation loans, rent-to-own services, pawn shops loans, or auto title loans. Underbanked rates from the three surveys are not directly comparable because of changes in the definition of underbanked households in both 2011 and 2013.

[3] All reported differences resulting from direct comparisons described in the text are statistically significant at the 10 percent level unless otherwise noted. In this case, the 2009 and 2013 estimates are each significantly different from 2011 but not from each other.

conditions and demographic composition of households over this period.

- In particular, compared to 2011, households in 2013 had slightly higher levels of employment and income, and were slightly older and better educated.[4] These characteristics are all associated with a higher likelihood of having a bank account.

- The highest unbanked rates continued to be found among non-Asian minorities, lower-income households, younger households, and unemployed households. Relative to 2011, the unbanked rates in 2013 were generally similar for these groups. One exception is Hispanic households.

  - While still relatively high, the unbanked rate for Hispanic households decreased to 17.9 percent in 2013 from 20.1 percent in 2011.

  - Improvements in economic conditions and changing demographics among Hispanic households over this period explain nearly half of the reduction in the unbanked rate among this population.

  - In particular, relative to 2011, Hispanic households in 2013 experienced higher levels of employment, income, and education. These characteristics are all associated with a higher likelihood of having a bank account.

- Among working-age disabled households, 18.4 percent were unbanked and 28.1 percent were underbanked in 2013.[5] This is the first time that the survey has reported estimates for these households.

---

[4] Household characteristics, such as race, age, education, and employment, are taken to be those of the owner or renter of the home (i.e., "householder"), unless the characteristic is one defined at the household level, such as income or household type. For convenience, some abbreviated language will be used to refer to these household characteristics. For example, the term "black household" refers to a household for which the householder has been identified as black. Note that other members of a household could have different characteristics from those of the householder. For instance, an unemployed household is defined as a household whose householder is unemployed, but other household members could be employed and earning income. The income measures included in this report reflect the income earned by all household members and not only the householder.

[5] Working-age is considered to be between age 25 and 64. Consistent with our approach for other household characteristics such as employment status, we classify a household as one with disabilities based on the characteristics of the owner or renter of the home (i.e., "householder"). Please refer to Appendix I for a detailed discussion of how we classified households as disabled.

Checking and Savings Account Ownership, and Automatic Transfers

Checking and savings account ownership rates remained similar to previous years. For the first time, the survey asked about automatic transfers, finding that most households use them primarily in connection with checking accounts.

- The vast majority of all U.S. households (88.4 percent) owned a checking account in 2013, while less than seven in ten (68.8 percent) owned a savings account.

- Four in five (80.3 percent) banked households had money directly deposited into a bank account or automatically transferred funds between accounts:

  - 94.5 percent of these households directly deposited or automatically transferred funds into checking accounts and 17.3 percent into savings accounts.[6]

  - Among the subset of households with savings accounts, 22.0 percent direct deposited or automatically transferred funds into a savings account.

Household Banking Status Transitions

For the first time, the survey asked households about both recent entrances and exits from the banking system as well as the circumstances affecting those transitions. Overall, economic events and motivations, such as job loss or opening an account to receive direct deposits, are found to have a stronger effect on banking status transitions than changes in household structure, such as marriage.

- Consistent with previous survey results, slightly less than half (45.9 percent) of unbanked households in 2013 were previously banked, which represented 3.6 percent of all U.S. households.

- In 2013, 0.7 percent of all U.S. households (or almost one in ten unbanked households) became unbanked within the last 12 months, while 1.6 percent became banked in the last 12 months.

---

[6] 13.2 percent of these direct deposits or transfers were to both checking and savings accounts. As a result, the total does not sum to 100 percent.

Figure ES.2 Previous Banking Status Of Unbanked Households

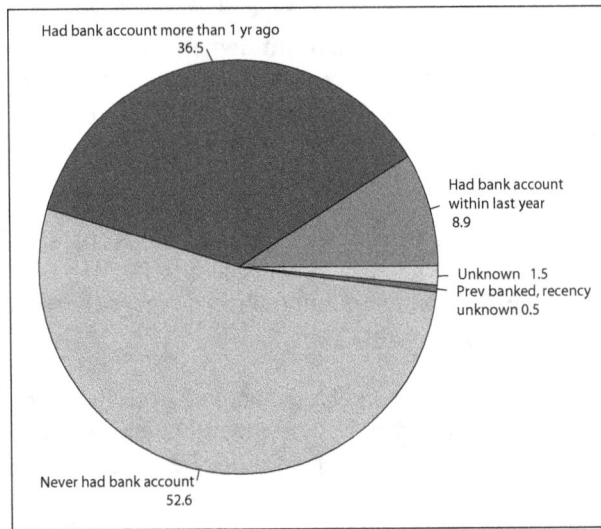

Had bank account more than 1 yr ago
36.5

Had bank account within last year
8.9

Unknown 1.5
Prev banked, recency unknown 0.5

Never had bank account
52.6

- While relatively small proportions of U.S. households experienced major life events in the past year, households that transitioned in or out of the banking system were more likely to have experienced certain events:

    - Among households that recently became unbanked, 34.1 percent experienced either a significant income loss or a job loss that they said contributed to the household becoming unbanked.

    - Among households that recently became banked, 19.4 percent reported that a new job contributed to their opening a bank account.

- About one-third (34.2 percent) of recently banked households also reported that receiving direct deposits was the main reason they opened an account. This was the most frequently reported reason, followed by "paying for everyday purchases, writing checks and/or paying bills," reported by one-quarter (25.0 percent) of recently banked households.

Reasons Households Were Unbanked

Unbanked households cited both economic and attitudinal reasons for remaining outside the banking system.

- A majority (57.5 percent) of unbanked households reported not having enough money to keep in an account or meet a minimum balance as one

reason they did not have an account and slightly more than a third (35.6 percent) of all unbanked households reported this to be the main reason.

- Roughly one in three (34.2 percent) unbanked households reported their dislike of or distrust in banks as one reason they were unbanked and slightly more than one in seven (14.9 percent) unbanked households reported this to be the main reason.

- Almost one in three unbanked households (30.8 percent) reported high or unpredictable account fees as one reason they did not have accounts and about 13 percent (13.4 percent) of unbanked households reported this to be the main reason.

    - Previously banked households (almost one in five or 17.7 percent) were more likely to say high or unpredictable fees were the main reason they were unbanked compared with households that never had an account (one in ten or 9.8 percent).

Future Banking Plans of Unbanked Households

Higher proportions of households that previously had an account reported being likely to open one in the next 12 months compared with households that had never been banked. How long ago a household last had a bank account also appeared to be correlated with intentions to rejoin the banking system. These results suggest that many consumers who have had experience, especially recent experience, with a bank account find value in having one.

- Almost half (48.6 percent) of unbanked households that previously had an account expressed an intention to open another in the next 12 months compared with only about one-quarter (25.2 percent) of households that had never been banked.

- Almost three out of four (74.8 percent) unbanked households that recently had a bank account, and 42.7 percent of unbanked households that had an account more than a year ago, reported being somewhat or very likely to open another in the next 12 months.

Figure ES.3 Reasons Households Were Unbanked

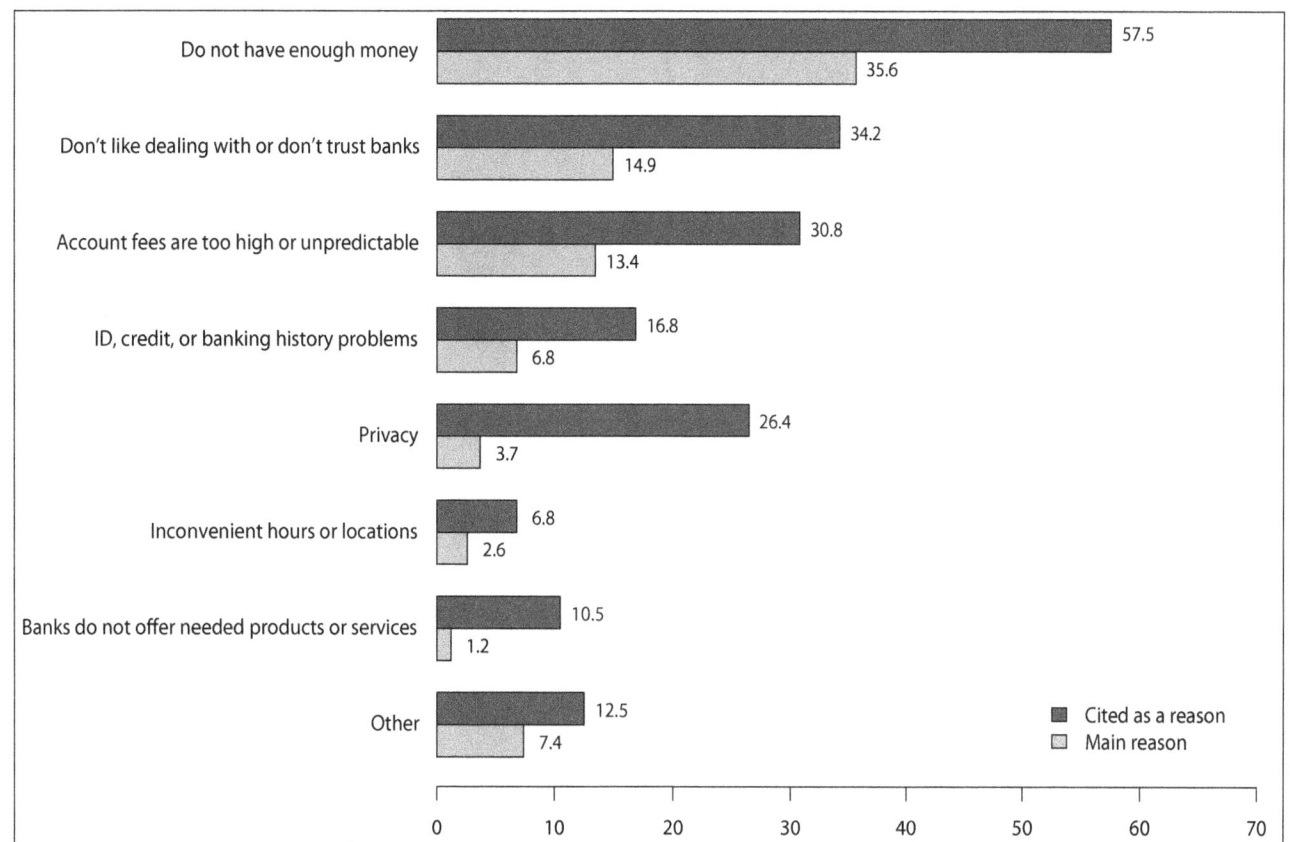

	Cited as a reason	Main reason
Do not have enough money	57.5	35.6
Don't like dealing with or don't trust banks	34.2	14.9
Account fees are too high or unpredictable	30.8	13.4
ID, credit, or banking history problems	16.8	6.8
Privacy	26.4	3.7
Inconvenient hours or locations	6.8	2.6
Banks do not offer needed products or services	10.5	1.2
Other	12.5	7.4

Prepaid Debit Card Use

Prepaid debit cards have emerged in recent years as a new payment method that some consumers use to address their financial transaction needs. Similar to a checking account, these cards can be used to pay bills, withdraw cash at ATMs, make purchases, deposit checks, and receive direct deposits. Many, although not all, such cards store funds in accounts eligible for deposit insurance. The survey results suggest that sizeable proportions of unbanked households and, to a lesser degree, underbanked households, relied on prepaid cards for many of the same purposes that households associate with checking accounts. Moreover, while some fully banked households used prepaid cards, unbanked and underbanked households accounted for a majority of prepaid card users.

- Nearly eight percent (7.9) of all households used prepaid cards in the last 12 months.

  - Unbanked households had the highest rate of use: 22.3 percent of unbanked households used a prepaid card in the last 12 months, compared with 13.1 percent of underbanked households and 5.3 percent of fully banked households.

  - Within the group of unbanked households, recently unbanked households had the highest rate of prepaid card use: 28.8 percent of this subset used a prepaid card in the last 12 months, compared with 22.0 percent of longer-term unbanked households.

- The highest rate of growth in prepaid card use was among unbanked households: In 2013, more than a quarter (27.1 percent) of unbanked households reported having ever used a prepaid card, up from 17.8 percent in 2011 and 12.2 percent in 2009.

- Unbanked prepaid card users appeared to more actively use their prepaid cards compared with other prepaid card users:

  - They were more likely to have reloaded their prepaid cards in the past 12 months (57.8 percent), relative to underbanked (42.9 percent) and fully banked (23.4 percent) households.

Figure ES.4 Banking Status Of Households That Used Prepaid Cards In The Last 12 Months

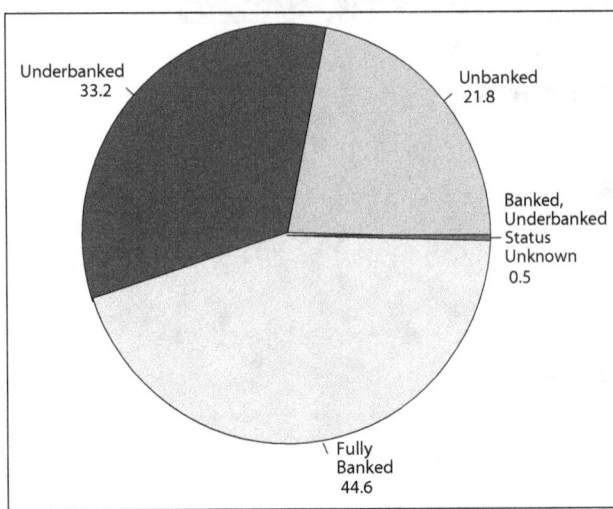

Underbanked 33.2

Unbanked 21.8

Banked, Underbanked Status Unknown 0.5

Fully Banked 44.6

Figure ES.5 Banking Status Of Households That Used Prepaid Cards In The Last 30 Days

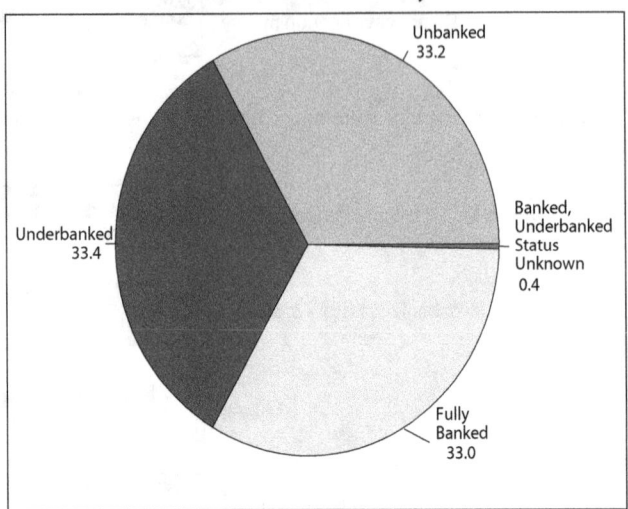

Unbanked 33.2

Underbanked 33.4

Banked, Underbanked Status Unknown 0.4

Fully Banked 33.0

• Unbanked households were also about two and a half times more likely to have used a prepaid card in the last 30 days (16.8 percent) compared with underbanked households (6.6 percent) and almost nine times more likely than fully banked households (1.9 percent).

• A much higher proportion of unbanked households that used prepaid cards in the last 12 months reported doing so primarily to meet their financial transaction needs. Specifically, 79.4 percent of these households cited "to pay for every day purchases or bills" or "to receive payments" as the main reason for using a prepaid card, compared with 53.3 percent of underbanked and 37.6 percent of fully banked households that used prepaid cards in the same period.

• A majority of prepaid card users were unbanked and underbanked households. More than half (55.0 percent) of the households that used prepaid cards in the last 12 months and about two-thirds (66.6 percent) of the households that used prepaid cards in the last 30 days were unbanked or underbanked.

• Almost half (46.5 percent) of unbanked households that used prepaid cards in the last 12 months reported being "very likely" or "somewhat likely" to open a bank account in the next 12 months, compared with 32.6 percent of unbanked households that had not used prepaid cards.

• Relatively few households (one in ten or 10.7 percent) that used prepaid cards obtained their

card from a bank branch. Among households that used prepaid cards, fully banked households were the most likely (15.4 percent) to have obtained their cards from a bank branch, while unbanked households were least likely (4.2 percent) to have done so.

Alternative Financial Services Use

One in four households reported obtaining either financial transaction services or credit from non-bank providers in the prior 12 months.[7] Households overall reported that "grocery, liquor, convenience, or drug stores" were the most common locations for obtaining transaction alternative financial services (AFS), but unbanked households were more likely to obtain these services from standalone AFS providers.

• Consistent with previous survey findings, about one in four households (24.9 percent) used at least one AFS in the previous 12 months, and 12.0 percent of all households used an AFS in the last 30 days.

  • Transaction AFS products, used by 21.9 percent of all households in the last 12 months, continue to be more widely used than credit AFS products, which were used by 7.0 percent of all households.

---

[7] The 2013 survey asks about non-bank use of three transaction products (money orders, check cashing, remittances) and five credit products (payday loans, pawn shop, refund anticipation loans, rent-to-own services, and auto title loans). Auto title loans were first asked about in the 2013 survey, so the AFS use estimates in this report are not directly comparable to estimates in past reports.

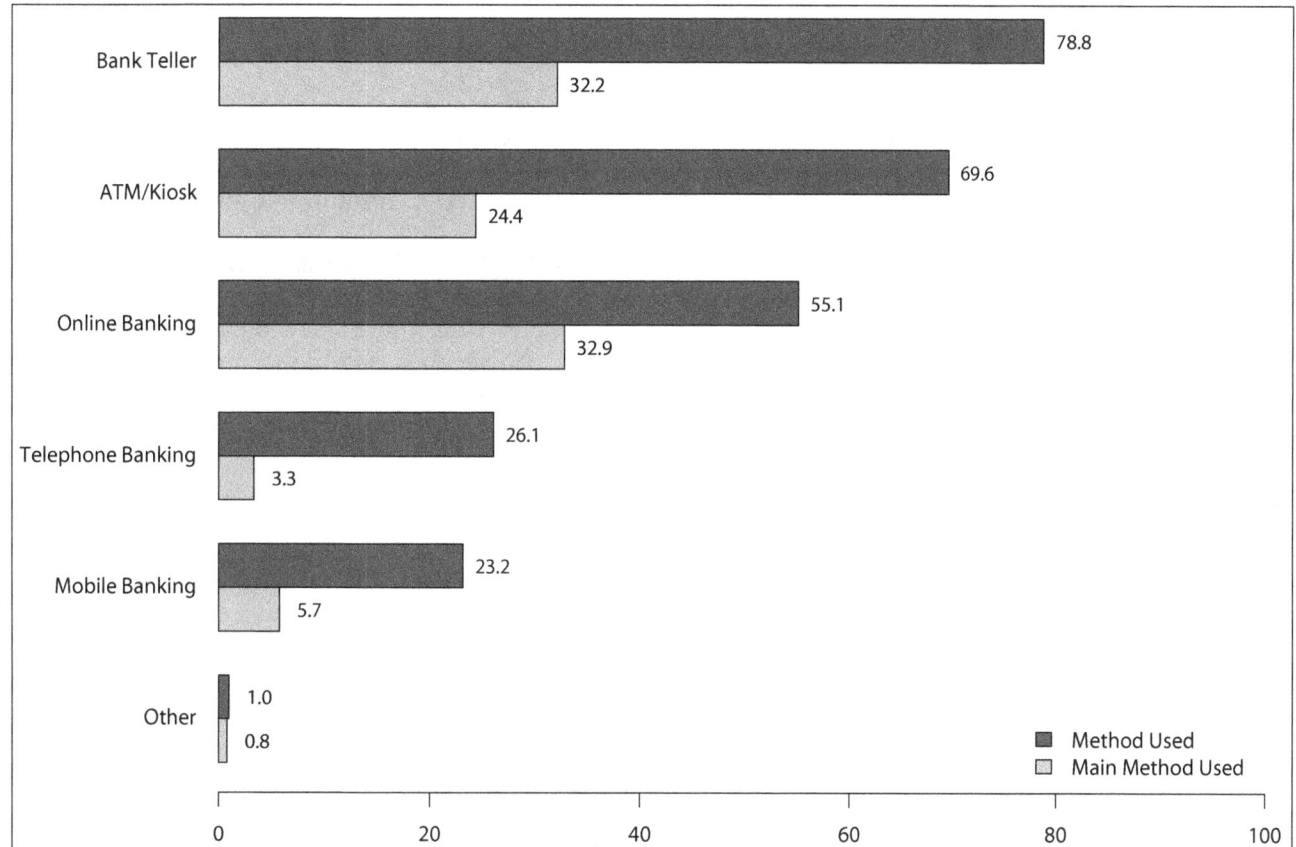

Figure ES.6 Methods Used To Access Bank Accounts In The Last 12 Months

	Method Used	Main Method Used
Bank Teller	78.8	32.2
ATM/Kiosk	69.6	24.4
Online Banking	55.1	32.9
Telephone Banking	26.1	3.3
Mobile Banking	23.2	5.7
Other	1.0	0.8

- AFS use continues to be relatively high among unbanked households: 63.2 percent used an AFS in the last 12 months, and 47.0 percent used an AFS in the last 30 days.

- The most common locations from which households obtained transaction AFS were "grocery, liquor, convenience, or drug stores."

  - For example, among households that used non-bank check cashing, 37.8 percent did so at a "grocery, liquor, convenience, or drug store" while 31.4 percent used a large retail or department store and 24.3 percent cashed their checks at standalone AFS providers.

- Among transaction AFS users, unbanked households were more likely than underbanked households to use stand-alone AFS providers. For example, 29.3 percent of unbanked households that used non-bank check cashing went to stand-alone AFS providers, compared to 20.6 percent of underbanked non-bank check cashing users.

Methods of Banking

For the first time, the 2013 survey examines the various ways households access their bank accounts.[8] The results show that bank tellers and online banking were the primary methods relied on by the largest share of banked households – about one-third of banked households primarily used bank tellers and another third primarily used online banking. Underbanked households were less likely to use online banking as their primary means of access, but were more likely to use mobile devices as a primary method. For those that did primarily use electronic means (online or mobile device) to access their account, most used at least two additional methods and many also reported using a teller. These results suggest that electronic means of access continue to be a supplement rather than a wholesale substitute for tellers.

---

[8] The survey asks whether the household used any of the following methods to access their account in the past 12 months: bank tellers, ATMs/kiosks, online banking, mobile banking, or telephone banking.

- Most banked households (71.1 percent) used multiple methods to access their bank accounts.[9]

- Many households used bank tellers to access their bank account. Nearly four out of five households (78.8 percent) used a bank teller in the past 12 months, one in three (32.2 percent) used bank tellers as their primary method of account access, and 17.5 percent used bank tellers as their only method of account access.

    - Roughly half (54.7 percent) of households age 65 or older, 55.7 percent of households without a high school degree, and 47.5 percent of households with annual income under $15,000 primarily used bank tellers to access their account.

- Use of online banking was also quite common. Over half (55.1 percent) of banked households accessed their account online in the past 12 months, and one in three (32.9 percent) used online banking as their primary means of account access. Underbanked households were less likely to have used online banking as their main banking method (26.6 percent) compared with fully banked households (35.1 percent).

- Among households that primarily used either online or mobile banking, use of additional methods was common. For example, households that primarily used online banking used a median of two additional methods to access their account while those that primarily relied on mobile banking used a median of three additional methods. One commonly used additional method was bank tellers, which were used by more than 70 percent of both groups.

Use of Mobile Technology and Mobile Banking

A majority of households reported having access to smartphones, and almost one in four reported using those devices to engage in mobile banking in the prior 12 months.[10] While a significant share of unbanked households had access to smartphones, their access lagged the population as a whole. In contrast, underbanked households were both more

likely to have access to smartphones than the general population and to have used them to engage in mobile banking.

- The vast majority of households (82.7 percent) had access to a mobile phone, of which two thirds (67.4 percent of all with mobile phone access or 55.7 percent overall) were smartphones.

    - Relative to fully banked households (86.8 percent), underbanked households were somewhat more likely to have had access to mobile phones (90.5 percent) and smartphones (64.5 percent of underbanked households compared with 59.0 percent of fully banked households).

    - Notably smaller, but still significant, proportions of unbanked households had access to mobile phones (68.1 percent) and smartphones (33.1 percent).

- Overall, 23.2 percent of banked households used mobile banking in the last 12 months, and a greater share of underbanked households (29.2 percent) than fully banked households (21.7 percent) had used mobile banking.

- Among mobile banking users, underbanked households were considerably more likely (32.4 percent) than the fully banked (21.6 percent) to use mobile banking as their main banking method. In contrast, fully banked mobile banking users were significantly more likely (54.2 percent) to use online banking as their main banking method than the underbanked (38.1 percent).

- Monitoring of account balance or recent transactions was the most common mobile banking activity (86.0 percent of mobile banking users). Only a quarter (25.5 percent) of households that used mobile banking used it to deposit a check. Underbanked households were more likely (51.5 percent) to have used mobile text alerts than fully banked households (44.6 percent).

Implications

The survey results presented in this report suggest implications for policymakers, financial institutions and other stakeholders who are working to improve access to mainstream financial services.

1. **Entrances and exits from the banking system are often associated with changes in employment**

---

[9] About 5 percent of banked households reported not having accessed their bank account in the past 12 months or did not report whether they had accessed their account in the last 12 months. These households are excluded from the estimates of bank account access presented here.

[10] Mobile banking was defined in the 2013 survey questionnaire as using text messages, mobile apps, or using a mobile phone's Internet browser or email to access a bank account.

and income. **Interventions designed to help households maintain and renew their banking relationships through economic challenges may reduce unbanked rates over time.**

Banking status is dynamic: many households cycle in and out of the banking system. For these households, financial life events, such as job loss, significant income loss, or a new job, appear to be important explanations for why they enter or exit the banking system.

Stakeholders might consider ways to cushion the impact of adverse financial shocks on a household's ability or desire to maintain a bank account. In particular, opportunities may exist for forbearance of fees, flexible product design, or direct interventions. Interventions could include targeted outreach or financial education for recently unemployed households to encourage them to remain in the banking system, for example.

The most frequently reported reason recently banked households cited for opening an account was to receive direct deposits. This finding suggests that opportunities may exist for bringing newly employed consumers into the financial mainstream by educating them on the use of bank accounts and on personal financial management. Opportunities also may exist to reach out to employers that do not yet offer direct deposit to help them lower costs and help their employees better understand opportunities offered by the mainstream banking system.

2. **Unbanked households are increasingly turning to general purpose reloadable prepaid cards to address their financial transaction needs and are generally obtaining them at non-bank locations. Opportunities may exist to meet these consumers' needs within the banking system.**

Prepaid card use is higher among unbanked households than other banking status groups, and has been growing rapidly. Although many unbanked prepaid card users, like other unbanked households, feel that they cannot have a bank account because they "do not have enough money to keep in an account or meet a minimum balance" or because "bank fees are too high or unpredictable," these households do have financial transaction needs. Many unbanked prepaid card users are using non-bank prepaid cards, instead of banking services, to make and receive payments. Banking products such as a low-cost, safe transaction account or a bank prepaid debit card that meets the specifications of the FDIC Safe Accounts Template

could help meet these financial needs while building banking relationships.[11]

In addition, many prepaid card users have prior experience with banking services and are relatively more inclined to enter a banking relationship going forward. Specifically, unbanked prepaid card users are more likely than nonusers to have had a bank account in the past, and to say they are likely to open an account in the future. This implies that, relative to other unbanked households, unbanked prepaid card users may be particularly receptive to entering or rejoining the banking system.

3. **Mobile banking is a potential tool to expand economic inclusion but branches continue to play an important role for many consumers, including those who are underbanked.**

Mobile banking has the potential to help expand economic inclusion. Mobile technologies provide the anytime, anyplace convenience that is highly valued by underserved consumers. The survey results show that mobile and smartphones are accessible to underserved populations, and that many underbanked households are already using mobile banking. Smartphones are more prevalent among underbanked households than among the fully banked. Underbanked households also are more likely than fully banked households to use mobile banking and more likely to use it as their primary banking channel.

Mobile technologies might also become useful tools for bringing unbanked households into the financial mainstream. While mobile phone ownership is less common among unbanked households than among the underbanked and fully banked, it is still sizable. Innovations such as mobile account opening could play a role in expanding access to banking for the unbanked.

In order for mobile banking to help promote economic inclusion, it is important that mobile banking offerings be designed and implemented in ways that are accessible and beneficial to the underserved. For example, to fully avail themselves of mobile banking opportunities, users must often have access to an online banking account. This could prevent underserved consumers who cannot or do not wish to use online banking from accessing and enjoying the benefits of mobile banking services.

---

[11] The FDIC Model Safe Accounts template provides insured institutions with guidelines on offering cost-effective transaction and savings accounts that are safe and affordable for consumers. See https://www.fdic.gov/consumers/template/.

Notably, the rise of mobile banking as a channel has not rendered other modes of banking unimportant, and non-mobile channels should continue to have a role in economic inclusion and outreach efforts. Other banking modes continue to be widely used by both underbanked and fully banked households. Traditional banking channels, such as branches, provide functions not commonly available through online and mobile banking. In particular, FDIC pilot studies have found that branch staff play an important role in making consumers aware of products, providing basic financial education, and growing their banking relationships.[12] As banking technologies continue to evolve, it is important to continue tracking how households access banking services, and to assess opportunities to increase banking engagement with underserved consumers across all relevant channels.

---

[12] Rae-Ann Miller, Susan Burhouse, Luke Reynolds and Aileen Sampson, "A Template for Success: The FDIC's Small Dollar Loan Pilot Program," FDIC Quarterly 2010, Volume 4, No. 2 and Sherrie Rhine and Susan Burhouse, "FDIC Model Safe Accounts Pilot: Final Report," April 2012.

2. Background and Objectives

A. Background

When households open an account at a federally insured depository institution, they establish a mainstream banking relationship. This relationship provides opportunities for households to deposit funds securely, conduct basic financial transactions, accumulate savings, and access credit on fair and affordable terms.

Despite these benefits, many households—referred to in this report as "unbanked"—do not have an account at an insured institution. Additional households have an account, but have also obtained financial services and products from non-bank, alternative financial services (AFS) providers in the prior 12 months. These households are referred to here as "underbanked." The existence of unbanked and underbanked households presents an opportunity for banks to expand access to their products and services and forge relationships with these underserved groups, ultimately increasing economic inclusion.

The FDIC recognizes that public confidence in the banking system is strengthened when banks effectively serve the broadest possible set of consumers. As a result, the agency is committed to increasing the participation of unbanked and underbanked households in the financial mainstream by ensuring that all Americans have access to safe, secure, and affordable banking services. The FDIC National Survey of Unbanked and Underbanked Households represents one contribution to this end.

Conducted to assess the inclusiveness of the banking system, and in partial response to a statutory mandate, this biennial survey provides estimates of unbanked and underbanked populations.[1] It also seeks to provide insights that will inform efforts to better meet the needs of these consumers.

The FDIC conducts the household survey in partnership with the U.S. Census Bureau. Specifically, the FDIC sponsors a special supplement on unbanked and underbanked households that is administered in conjunction with Census Bureau's Current Population Survey (CPS).

This report presents the results of the 2013 FDIC National Survey of Unbanked and Underbanked Households. The survey was conducted in June 2013 and collected responses from 40,998 households[2] (see FDIC Technical Note in Appendix I for additional details).

The results of this survey complement other FDIC efforts and initiatives to increase sustainable and safe access to the financial mainstream. For more information on those efforts and for additional resources from this survey, including the ability to query the underlying data, readers should visit http://www. economicinclusion.gov.

The first FDIC National Survey of Unbanked and Underbanked Households was conducted in January 2009, and the second survey was conducted in June 2011. Results from the 2009 and 2011 surveys are also available at http://www.economicinclusion.gov.

The FDIC encourages researchers, policy makers, consumer and community groups, and financial institutions to use the publicly available data to improve understanding of the issues and challenges underserved households perceive when deciding how and where to conduct financial transactions. The information provided in this report, as well future analysis produced with the publicly available data, will contribute to efforts to create sustainable banking opportunities for a broad set of consumers.

B. What's New

Revisions to the 2013 Survey Instrument

The 2013 survey instrument is similar to the 2011 survey. However, a few important changes were made to provide greater insight into the circumstances of unbanked and underbanked households. The details

---

[1] The household survey is a key component of the FDIC's efforts to comply with a congressional mandate contained in section 7 of the Federal Deposit Insurance Reform Conforming Amendments Act of 2005 (Pub. L. 109–173), which calls for the FDIC to conduct ongoing surveys, "on efforts by insured depository institutions to bring those individuals and families who have rarely, if ever, held a checking account, a savings account or other type of transaction or check cashing account at an insured depository institution ('unbanked') into the conventional finance system." Section 7 further instructs the FDIC to consider several factors when conducting the surveys, including estimating the size and worth of the unbanked market in the United States and identifying the primary issues that prevent unbanked individuals from establishing conventional accounts.

[2] A total of 53,405 households participated in the June 2013 Current Population Survey. Of these households, 40,998 (77 percent) also participated in the Unbanked/Underbanked Supplement.

of these changes, summarized below, are provided in Appendix J.

The changes to the 2013 survey instrument broadly fall into five areas:

First, questions were added to explore household exits from and entrances into the banking system over the prior year and whether major financial and non-financial life events were associated with these entrances and exits. A new question also asked recent entrants about reasons for opening an account that were not related to a life event. And existing questions on the reasons households were unbanked were revised.

Second, questions on direct deposits and automatic transfers into bank accounts were added to provide greater detail about the use of automatic transfers into different account types by households with different characteristics.

Third, questions were added to better understand households' use of general purpose reloadable prepaid debit cards, an emerging payment instrument. Many, although not all, such cards store funds in accounts eligible for deposit insurance, and some of these cards are issued directly by banks to consumers.

Fourth, questions on households' use of auto title loans were added and use of these loans was one type of Alternative Financial Service (AFS) used to identify underbanked households in the 2013 report. In addition, questions were added on the locations from which households obtained transaction AFS products.

Finally, questions were added to explore households' access to and use of technology such as smartphones, which could provide additional opportunities to establish and deepen banking relationships. In part, to place answers to those questions in context, questions were also added on the broader set of methods that households used to access their bank accounts.

While differences over time in survey results are of interest, comparability of the 2013 results to certain 2009 and 2011 estimates is limited or not possible due to differences across the surveys. For example, underbanked estimates are not comparable across the three surveys due to different types of AFS that were used in each year to identify underbanked households.

3. Banking Status of U.S. Households

In 2013, an estimated 7.7 percent of households in the United States (approximately one in thirteen households) did not have a checking or savings account and, for the purposes of this report, are considered unbanked. This proportion represented nearly 9.6 million households in which approximately 16.7 million adults and 8.7 million children lived.[1]

An additional 20.0 percent (24.8 million) of U.S. households had a bank account but also used alternative financial services (AFS) outside of the banking system. For the purposes of this report, these households are considered underbanked. Underbanked households are defined as those households that had a checking or savings account or both, and had used at least one of the following AFS from non-bank providers in the last 12 months: money orders, check cashing, remittances, payday loans, refund anticipation loans, rent-to-own services, pawn shops loans, or auto title loans.[2] Approximately 50.9 million adults and 16.6 million children lived in underbanked households in 2013.[3] Approximately 5.3 percent of U.S. households were banked but information about their use of AFS was insufficient to determine whether they were underbanked.

Most households in the United States (67.0 percent) had at least one bank account and had not, in the past 12 months, used any of the types of AFS included in the survey.[4] These households are considered fully banked.

Figure 3.1 Banking Status Of U.S. Households

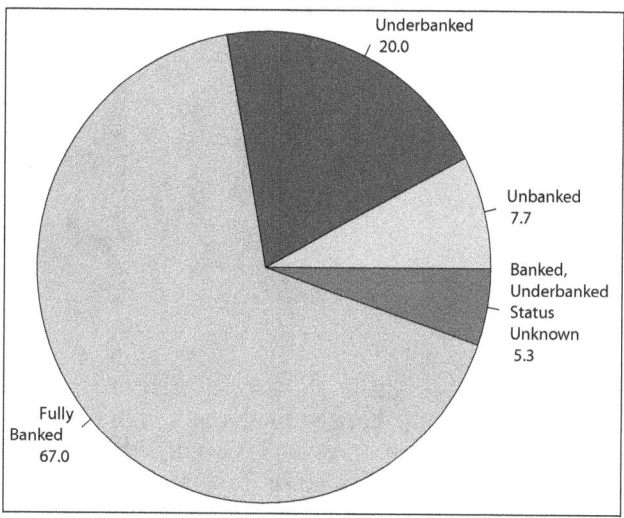

Changes in Banking Status 2009-2013

The unbanked rate has varied from 7.6 percent in 2009 to 8.2 percent in 2011 to 7.7 in 2013.[5] The decrease in the unbanked rate between 2011 and 2013 can be explained by differences in the economic conditions and demographic composition of households over this period.[6] In particular, compared to 2011, households in 2013 had slightly higher levels of employment and income, and were slightly older and better educated. These characteristics are all associated with lower unbanked rates.[7]

---

[1] Adults are defined as people age 16 and older. This is a lower-bound estimate of the number of unbanked adults in the United States because it is based on the assumption that all adults residing in a "banked" household are banked in the sense that they may benefit from the account. A banked household may have one or more unbanked adults; these unbanked adults residing in banked households are not included in the 16.7 million adults figure cited in this report.

[2] Auto title loans are loans in which consumers borrow using as collateral the title of the car or cars that they own. These are not loans used to purchase an automobile.

[3] This is an upper-bound estimate of the total number of underbanked adults in the United States because it is based on the assumption that all adults residing in an underbanked household are underbanked. However, an underbanked household may have one or more adults who are not underbanked.

[4] Fully banked households may have never used AFS, used AFS more than a year ago, or may have, in the past 12 months, used types of AFS not included in this survey.

[5] All reported differences resulting from direct comparisons described in the text are statistically significant at the 10 percent level unless otherwise noted. In this case, the 2009 and 2013 estimates are each significantly different from the 2011 estimate but not from each other.

[6] Differences in the economic conditions and demographic composition of households in the 2011 and 2013 surveys account for about 80 percent of the difference in the unbanked rates across these two years. After accounting for these differences, the 2011 and 2013 unbanked rates are no longer statistically significantly different from each other.

[7] For example, 29.0 percent of households in the 2013 survey had incomes of at least $75,000 compared with 26.6 percent of households in the 2011 survey. And 15.4 percent of households in the 2013 survey had incomes of less than $15,000 compared with 16.2 percent of households in the 2011 survey. In 2013, 0.5 percent of households with incomes of at least $75,000 were unbanked and 27.7 percent of households with incomes of less than $15,000 were unbanked. Because of such large differences in unbanked rates across income groups, the differences in income between the 2011 and 2013 surveys explain a portion of the difference in the overall unbanked rates between 2011 and 2013.

Figure 3.2 Unbanked Households By Year

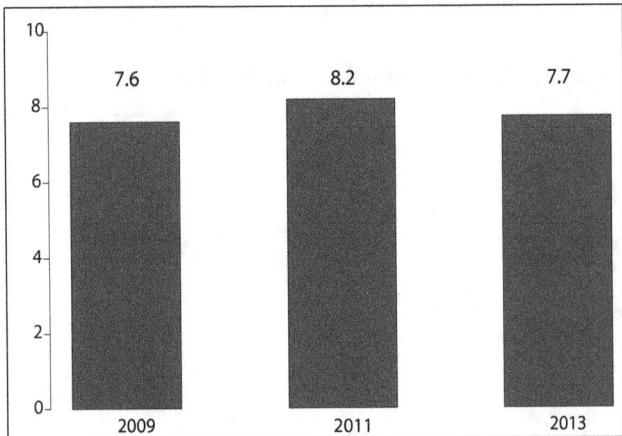

Underbanked rates from the three surveys are not directly comparable because of changes in the definition of underbanked households in both 2011 and 2013. In 2013, the definition of underbanked includes the use of auto title loans, which was not considered in 2011. Including the use of auto title loans has a very small effect on the share of underbanked households – it increases the underbanked rate by 0.3 percentage points. Excluding the use of auto title

loans, the 2013 underbanked rates remained at similar levels relative to 2011.[8]

Banking Status and Household Characteristics

The share of unbanked and underbanked households continued to vary significantly by households' socio-economic and demographic characteristics (see Appendix Table A-1a, included below).[9] The highest unbanked and underbanked rates were found among

[8] Excluding the use of auto title loans, the proportion of underbanked households decreased, from 20.1 percent in 2011 to 19.8 percent in 2013. However, relative to 2011, the proportion of unknown answers for most of the alternative financial services questions generally doubled, which resulted in a higher share of banked households whose underbanked status could not be determined (from 2.9 percent in 2011 to 5.2 percent in 2013 when excluding auto title loans). Excluding households with unknown underbanked status, the underbanked rate stayed relatively constant: 20.7 percent in 2011 and 20.9 percent in 2013. Regardless of whether unknowns are excluded, the difference in the underbanked rate between 2013 and 2011 is not statistically significant.

[9] Household characteristics, such as race, age, education, and employment, are taken to be those of the owner or renter of the home (i.e., "householder"), unless the characteristic is one defined at the household level, such as income or household type. For convenience, some abbreviated language will be used to refer to these household characteristics. For example, the term "black household" refers to a household for which the householder has been identified as black. Note that other members of a household could have different characteristics from those of the householder. For instance, an unemployed household is defined as a household whose householder is unemployed, but other household members could be employed and earning income. The income measures included in this report reflect the income earned by all household members and not only the householder.

Appendix Table A-1a Banking Status By Household Characteristics, 2013

For all households, row percent

Characteristics	Number of Households (1000s)	Percent of Households	Unbanked (Percent)	Banked: Underbanked (Percent)	Banked: Fully Banked (Percent)	Banked: Underbanked Status Unknown (Percent)
All	123,750	100	7.7	20.0	67.0	5.3
Household Type						
Married couple	59,102	100	3.4	17.7	73.9	5.0
Unmarried female-headed family	15,802	100	18.4	29.2	47.5	4.9
Unmarried male-headed family	6,327	100	13.2	28.3	53.7	4.8
Female individual	22,150	100	7.4	17.2	69.4	6.0
Male individual	20,240	100	10.7	20.0	63.7	5.7
Other	128	100	16.3	17.5	58.6	7.6
Race/Ethnicity						
Black	16,801	100	20.5	33.1	40.0	6.3
Hispanic	14,948	100	17.9	28.5	48.4	5.1
Asian	5,882	100	2.2	17.9	73.4	6.6
American Indian/Alaskan	1,464	100	16.9	25.5	53.0	4.6
Hawaiian/Pacific Islander	314	100	6.1	25.1	64.5	4.2
White non-Black non-Hispanic	84,310	100	3.6	15.9	75.4	5.0

Appendix Table A-1a Banking Status By Household Characteristics, 2013

For all households, row percent

Characteristics	Number of Households (1000s)	Percent of Households	Unbanked (Percent)	Banked: Underbanked (Percent)	Banked: Fully Banked (Percent)	Banked: Underbanked Status Unknown (Percent)
Other non-Black non-Hispanic	NA	NA	NA	NA	NA	NA
Spanish only language spoken						
Spanish is not the only language spoken	121,097	100	7.1	19.9	67.6	5.3
Spanish is only language spoken	2,654	100	34.9	23.7	38.1	3.3
Nativity						
U.S.-born	106,397	100	6.9	19.1	69.0	5.1
Foreign born citizen	9,252	100	4.7	24.0	64.6	6.7
Foreign born non citizen	8,102	100	22.7	28.0	43.9	5.4
Age Group						
15 to 24 years	6,244	100	15.7	30.8	48.8	4.6
25 to 34 years	20,464	100	12.5	24.7	58.3	4.6
35 to 44 years	21,408	100	9.0	23.8	62.5	4.6
45 to 54 years	24,551	100	7.5	21.9	65.4	5.2
55 to 64 years	22,710	100	5.6	17.7	71.7	5.0
65 years or more	28,372	100	3.5	11.6	78.2	6.7
Disability Status						
Disabled	10,841	100	18.4	28.1	49.0	4.5
Not Disabled	78,293	100	7.2	21.1	66.8	4.9
Not Applicable	34,616	100	5.7	15.1	72.9	6.3
Education						
No high school degree	13,871	100	25.1	24.1	46.3	4.6
High school degree	33,684	100	10.8	21.9	61.7	5.6
Some college	36,007	100	5.6	23.0	66.2	5.2
College degree	40,188	100	1.1	14.3	79.3	5.3
Employment Status						
Employed	75,587	100	5.4	21.7	67.8	5.0
Unemployed	5,436	100	23.0	25.3	47.8	3.8
Not in labor force	42,727	100	9.9	16.3	67.9	5.9
Family Income						
Less than $15,000	19,044	100	27.7	22.4	45.2	4.7
Between $15,000 and $30,000	21,763	100	11.4	25.0	57.9	5.7
Between $30,000 and $50,000	24,496	100	5.1	23.3	65.7	5.9
Between $50,000 and $75,000	22,552	100	1.7	19.8	73.2	5.2
At Least $75,000	35,895	100	0.5	13.6	81.0	4.9
Homeownership						
Homeowner	80,136	100	2.6	15.5	76.7	5.2
Non-homeowner	43,614	100	17.3	28.2	49.2	5.3
Geographic Region						
Northeast	22,199	100	6.8	19.3	68.4	5.5
Midwest	27,315	100	6.4	16.9	71.4	5.2
South	46,738	100	9.2	23.5	62.1	5.2
West	27,498	100	7.4	17.6	69.6	5.3

Appendix Table A-1a Banking Status By Household Characteristics, 2013

For all households, row percent

Characteristics	Number of Households (1000s)	Percent of Households	Unbanked (Percent)	Banked: Underbanked (Percent)	Banked: Fully Banked (Percent)	Banked: Underbanked Status Unknown (Percent)
Metropolitan Status						
Metropolitan area - Principal City	34,510	100	11.4	22.3	60.8	5.5
Metropolitan area - Balance	51,229	100	5.5	17.8	71.1	5.6
Not in Metropolitan area	19,325	100	8.5	21.0	66.1	4.5
Not Identified	18,686	100	6.4	20.8	68.1	4.8

NA= Not available because the sample size was too small to produce a precise estimate.

-= For this table cell, the estimated proportion would round to zero. The population proportion, however, is likely to be slightly greater than zero.

Figures do not always reconcile to totals because of rounding.

non-Asian minorities, lower-income households, younger households, unemployed households and working-age disabled households.[10] Close to half of all households in these groups were unbanked or underbanked compared to slightly more than one-quarter of all households.

Relative to 2011, the estimated unbanked rates in 2013 were generally similar for most groups.[11] One exception is Hispanic households. While still relatively high, the unbanked rate for Hispanic households decreased to 17.9 percent in 2013 from 20.1 percent in 2011. Improvements in economic conditions and changing demographics among Hispanic households over this time period explain nearly half of this reduction in the unbanked rate. In particular, relative to 2011, Hispanic households in 2013 experienced higher levels of employment, income and educational attainment. These characteristics are all associated with lower unbanked rates.

Banking Status and Geography

The share of unbanked and underbanked households varied substantially by geography. The regional variation in unbanked and underbanked rates in 2013 is consistent with previous survey results. The Southern region had the highest unbanked and underbanked rates (9.2 percent and 23.5 percent, respectively). In fact, while 38 percent of U.S. households live in the South, approximately 44 percent of unbanked and underbanked households lived there. The Midwest

region had the lowest unbanked and underbanked rates (6.4 percent and 16.9 percent). Unbanked rates ranged from 1.9 percent in Alaska to 14.5 percent in Mississippi, while underbanked rates were lowest in Wisconsin (10.4 percent) and highest in Mississippi (32.8 percent). Relative to 2011, four states experienced statistically significant declines in unbanked rates: Alaska (from 5.2 percent to 1.9 percent), North Dakota (from 5.3 percent to 2.8 percent), Texas (from 12.8 percent to 10.4 percent), and Michigan (from 7.7 percent to 5.7 percent).

Household Banking Status Transitions

The 2013 survey asked whether households experienced changes in banking status, including the timeframe in which they became banked or unbanked. We use these questions to examine the dynamic nature of household banking status.

Among unbanked households in 2013, consistent with previous survey results, slightly more than half (52.6 percent) had never been banked, which represented 4.1 percent of all U.S. households. However, for certain demographic groups, the share of unbanked households that had never had an account was disproportionately high. For example, 70.4 percent of unbanked Hispanic households never had an account (see Appendix Table A-4).

Slightly less than half (45.9 percent) of unbanked households in 2013 had a bank account in the past (previously banked households). Most of the previously banked households (79.5 percent) had been without an account for more than 12 months, while 19.4 percent (or 8.9 percent of all unbanked households) became unbanked more recently.[12]

---

[10] Working-age is considered to be between age 25 and 64. Consistent with our approach for other household characteristics such as employment status, we classify a household as one with disabilities based on the characteristics of the owner or renter of the home (i.e., "householder"). Please refer to Appendix I for a detailed discussion of how we classified households as disabled.

[11] Reported differences between groups described in the text are statistically significant at the 10% level in a model that includes the entire set of household characteristics listed in Appendix Table A-1.

[12] In comparison, in 2009, 28.1 percent of previously unbanked households were recently unbanked and in 2011, the comparable percentage was 20.3 percent.

Figure 3.3 Unbanked Rates By State, 2013

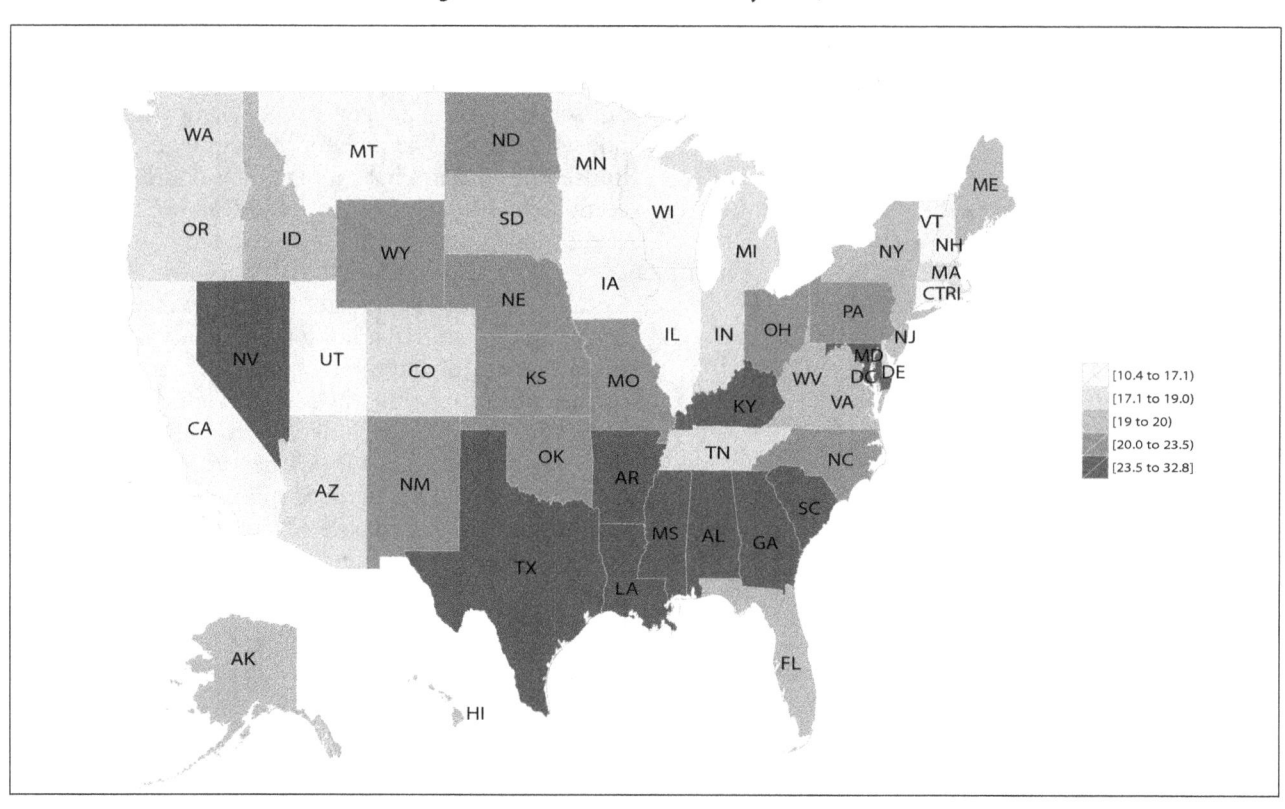

Legend:
- [1.9 to 4.5)
- [4.5 to 5.8)
- [5.8 to 7.4)
- [7.4 to 10.4)
- [10.4 to 14.5]

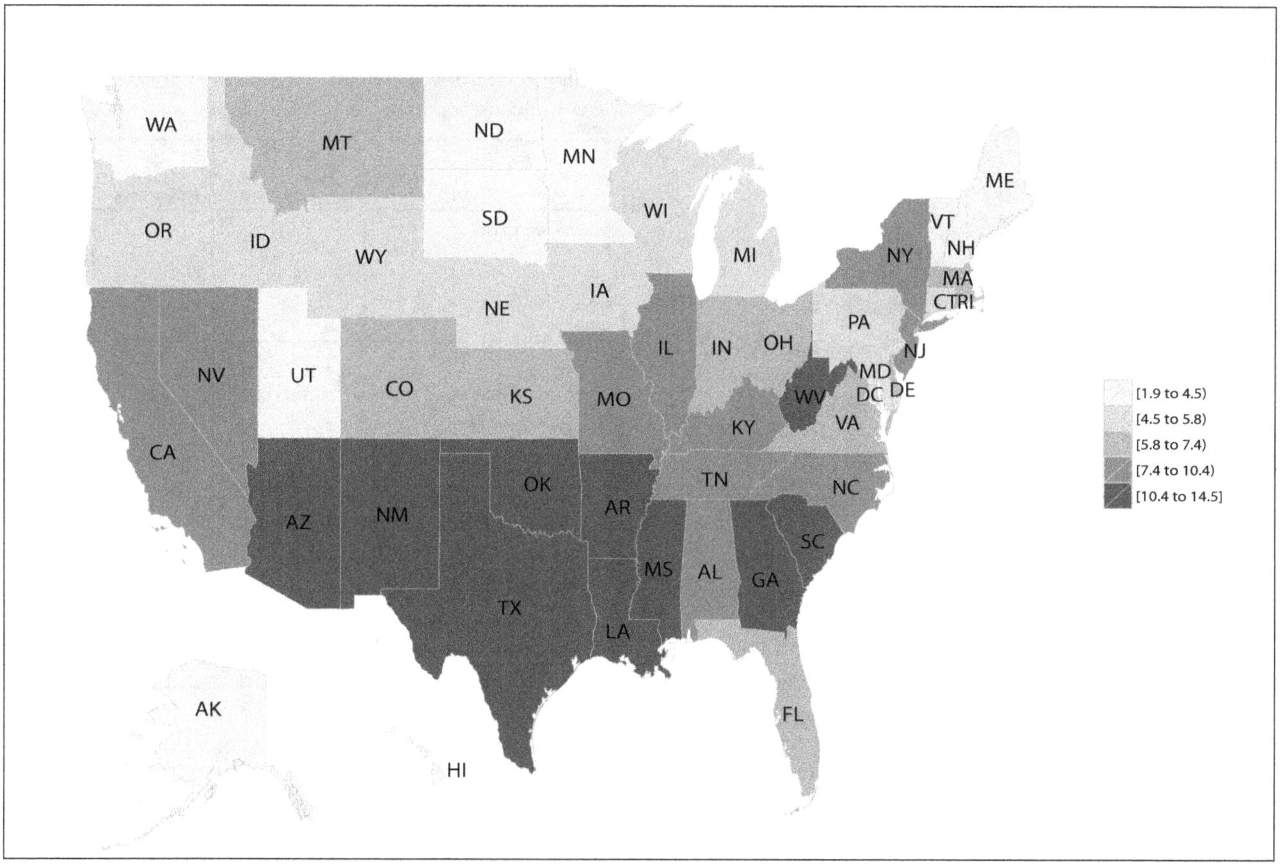

Figure 3.4 Underbanked Rates By State, 2013

Legend:
- [10.4 to 17.1)
- [17.1 to 19.0)
- [19 to 20)
- [20.0 to 23.5)
- [23.5 to 32.8]

Figure 3.5 Previous Banking Status Of Unbanked Households in 2013

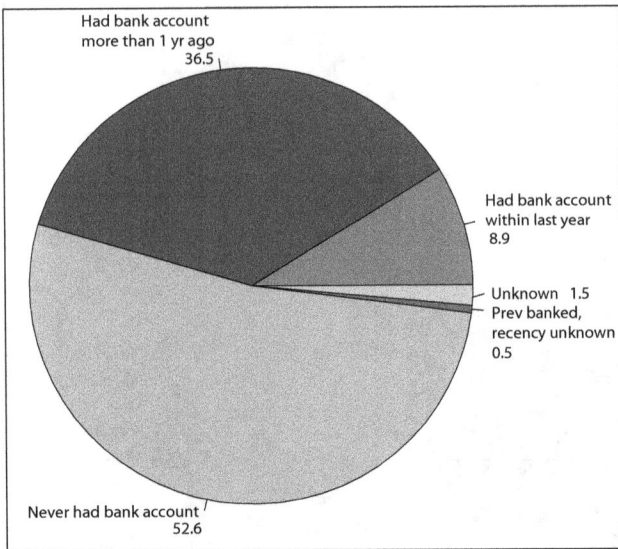

Had bank account more than 1 yr ago 36.5
Had bank account within last year 8.9
Unknown 1.5
Prev banked, recency unknown 0.5
Never had bank account 52.6

Focusing on whether households had experienced changes to their banking status over the past year, we classify households into one of four groups, as shown in Table 3.1.[13] Almost 7 percent (6.9 percent) of households were "longer-term unbanked", meaning they did not have a bank account in 2013 and also did not have a bank account within the last year.[14]

A small proportion of households, 0.7 percent, were "recently unbanked", meaning they did not have a bank account at the time of the 2013 survey, but had an account at some point within the last year. Almost one in ten unbanked households were "recently unbanked".

Another 1.6 percent of households were "recently banked", meaning they had an account in 2013, but at some point within the last 12 months no one in the household had an account. The remaining 90.9 percent of households were "longer-term banked", meaning they had an account in 2013, and had at least one bank account continuously for at least 12 months.

These results show that while the vast majority of households had been in their current banking status

for a year or more, a non-trivial number recently became banked or unbanked.

Table 3.1 Household Banking Status Transitions

For all housholds with non-missing recent bank status and non-missing life events.

	All	Longer-term Unbanked	Recently Unbanked	Recently Banked	Longer-term Banked
Number of House-holds (1000s)	115,872	7,973	807	1,800	105,292
Category as a share of all households	100	6.9	0.7	1.6	90.9

Banking Status Transitions and Household Characteristics

It is useful to understand how the socioeconomic and demographic characteristics of households differed across the four banking status transition categories. As illustrated in Appendix Table A-6b (included on the following page), relative to the longer-term banked, households that recently transitioned into or out of a mainstream bank account had higher proportions of certain socioeconomic and demographic characteristics that are associated with being unbanked.

For example, 48.0 percent of recently unbanked households and 32.4 percent of recently banked households had family income of less than $15,000. In contrast, 56.6 percent of longer-term unbanked households had income of less than $15,000, compared to only 11.6 percent of longer-term banked households. And 22.9 percent of recently unbanked households and 24.2 percent of recently banked households did not have a high-school diploma, compared with 38.2 percent of longer-term unbanked and 8.8 percent of longer-term banked households.

Certain household characteristics were disproportionately represented among the recently unbanked. In particular, the unemployment rate among recently unbanked households was 25.4 percent, substantially higher than among the longer-term unbanked (12.0 percent), recently banked (8.1 percent), and longer-term banked (3.6 percent). Similarly, 49.3 percent of recently-unbanked households were black, compared with 34.0 percent of longer-term unbanked, 25.0 percent of recently banked, and 11.2 percent of longer-term banked.

---

[13] The estimates presented in Tables 3.1, 3.2, 3.3 and Appendix Table A-6b are for households for which we have information on recent bank status and incidence of life events. Specifically, the estimates were computed excluding 882 observations (representing roughly 2.8 million households) removed due to missing information on recent banking status, and 1,602 additional observations (representing roughly 5.0 million households) removed due to missing data on the incidence of life events.

[14] Households that were "longer-term unbanked" may never have had an account or they may have had an account more than a year ago.

Appendix Table A-6b Household Characteristics By Banking Transitions, 2013

For all households with non-missing recent bank status and non-missing life events, column percent

Characteristics	All	Longer Term Unbanked	Recently Unbanked	Recently Banked	Longer Term Banked
Number of Households (1000s)	115,872	7,973	807	1,800	105,292
Percent of Households	100	100	100	100	100
Household Type (Percent)					
Married couple	48.2	21.1	23.6	33.8	50.7
Unmarried female-headed family	12.7	30.8	33.9	23.8	11.0
Unmarried male-headed family	5.2	9.0	8.9	9.1	4.8
Female individual	17.7	16.6	17.2	13.1	17.9
Male individual	16.1	22.3	16.4	20.1	15.6
Other	0.1	0.3	-	-	0.1
Race/Ethnicity (Percent)					
Black	13.2	34.0	49.3	25.0	11.2
Hispanic	12.1	29.5	18.4	22.8	10.5
Asian	4.7	1.3	0.1	5.1	5.0
American Indian/Alaskan	1.2	2.6	3.2	2.7	1.0
Hawaiian/Pacific Islander	0.3	0.2	-	0.2	0.3
White non-Black non-Hispanic	68.5	32.4	29.0	44.2	72.0
Other non-Black non-Hispanic	-	-	-	-	-
Spanish only language spoken (Percent)					
Spanish is not the only language spoken	97.9	89.7	96.3	93.7	98.6
Spanish is only language spoken	2.1	10.3	3.7	6.3	1.4
Nativity (Percent)					
U.S.-born	86.1	75.1	85.5	79.0	87.1
Foreign born citizen	7.4	4.6	4.3	8.8	7.6
Foreign born non citizen	6.5	20.3	10.2	12.2	5.3
Age Group (Percent)					
15 to 24 years	5.1	10.5	12.5	10.0	4.5
25 to 34 years	16.6	26.1	33.9	20.5	15.7
35 to 44 years	17.4	20.2	20.6	20.9	17.1
45 to 54 years	19.9	19.4	17.7	21.9	19.9
55 to 64 years	18.5	13.6	7.4	14.7	19.0
65 years or more	22.6	10.1	8.1	12.0	23.8
Disability Status (Percent)					
Disabled	8.7	21.3	14.7	17.3	7.6
Not Disabled	63.6	58.1	64.8	60.7	64.1
Not Applicable	27.6	20.6	20.5	22.0	28.3
Education (Percent)					
No high school degree	11.2	38.2	22.9	24.2	8.8
High school degree	27.1	38.1	36.3	34.2	26.0
Some college	29.1	19.4	36.9	29.6	29.8
College degree	32.7	4.3	4.0	12.1	35.4
Employment Status (Percent)					
Employed	61.4	43.1	43.8	60.0	63.0
Unemployed	4.4	12.0	25.4	8.1	3.6

Appendix Table A-6b Household Characteristics By Banking Transitions, 2013

For all households with non-missing recent bank status and non-missing life events, column percent

Characteristics	All	Longer Term Unbanked	Recently Unbanked	Recently Banked	Longer Term Banked
Not in labor force	34.2	45.0	30.9	31.9	33.4
Family Income (Percent)					
Less than $15,000	15.3	56.6	48.0	32.4	11.6
Between $15,000 and $30,000	17.4	25.2	29.9	28.9	16.6
Between $30,000 and $50,000	19.7	12.7	13.7	18.4	20.3
Between $50,000 and $75,000	18.3	3.5	8.0	8.1	19.7
At Least $75,000	29.3	2.0	0.4	12.2	31.9
Homeownership (Percent)					
Homeowner	65.0	20.8	19.2	39.6	69.1
Non-homeowner	35.0	79.2	80.8	60.4	30.9
Geographic Region (Percent)					
Northeast	17.9	15.9	15.0	18.6	18.0
Midwest	22.1	17.8	19.0	17.4	22.5
South	37.8	44.7	43.4	45.0	37.1
West	22.3	21.7	22.6	19.0	22.4
Metropolitan Status (Percent)					
Metropolitan area - Principal City	27.8	41.5	40.9	35.4	26.5
Metropolitan area - Balance	41.3	28.9	31.6	33.8	42.4
Not in Metropolitan area	15.8	17.1	14.5	16.0	15.7
Not Identified	15.2	12.5	12.9	14.7	15.4

NA= Not available because the sample size was too small to produce a precise estimate.

-= For this table cell, the estimated proportion would round to zero. The population proportion, however, is likely to be slightly greater than zero.

Figures do not always reconcile to totals because of rounding.

Banking Status Transitions and Incidence of Life Events

Different types of major life events experienced by recently unbanked and recently banked households may have contributed to the changes in these households' banking status. The 2013 survey asked new questions about major financial life events, which included significant income loss or gain, job loss or new job, significant increased or decreased expenses, and retirement. The 2013 survey also asked about major non-financial life events, including divorce or death, new marriage, birth, and moves. Households were asked if they had experienced any of these events, and recently unbanked and recently banked households were asked whether any events that they experienced contributed to them opening or closing their bank account.

Relatively small proportions of households experienced a life event in the past year, but some households were more likely to experience such an event than others. Table 3.2 shows the incidence of life events across the four banking status transition categories. Households that recently became banked or unbanked reported a relatively high incidence of financial life events, especially job and significant income changes, suggesting that such households also faced greater volatility in their employment status. For example, 38.1 percent of recently unbanked households and 30.7 percent of recently banked households experienced a significant loss of income in the last 12 months, compared with 25.1 percent of longer-term unbanked and 13.0 percent of longer term banked households.

The incidence of non-financial life events was generally small and relatively consistent across all four banking status transitions categories, with the exception of moves. Similar to the financial life events, moves or relocations were experienced by higher proportions of recently banked and recently unbanked households. Households that experienced moves were also likely to have experienced either changes in employment or significant changes in income.[15]

Table 3.2 Banking Status Transitions And Incidence Of Life Events

For all households with non-missing recent bank status and non-missing life events, column percent

Life Event	All	Longer-term Unbanked	Recently Unbanked	Recently Banked	Longer-term Banked
Job or Significant income loss	17.1	29.5	44.9	37.2	15.6
Significant income loss	14.3	25.1	38.1	30.7	13.0
Significant increase in income	5.8	4.3	6.4	7.3	5.9
Job loss	10.2	18.7	35.4	23.0	9.2
New job	13.0	11.5	19.3	26.6	12.9
Retirement	2.8	1.6	2.0	2.9	2.9
Significant increase in Household expenses	15.7	16.1	25.3	21.8	15.5
Significant decrease in Household expenses	2.2	3.6	5.7	4.5	2.0
Divorce or death	2.3	2.4	2.1	3.2	2.3
New marriage	1.7	1.6	2.4	2.5	1.7
Birth or adoption	3.1	4.8	6.3	3.7	2.9
Move or relocation	10.0	14.2	20.4	18.0	9.4

The relatively high incidence of adverse financial shocks among recently unbanked households suggests that such events may lead to bank account closure. The results also suggest that positive changes might be associated with bank account opening, as a higher proportion of recently banked households experienced a new job (26.6 percent) compared with households in the other three banking status transitions categories.[16]

To learn more about the possible causal linkages between life events and bank account openings and closings, the survey asked households not only whether they experienced the specified events but also whether any life event they experienced contributed to a change in banking status. These results are presented in Table 3.3, and provide additional evidence about the extent to which specific events may affect household decisions to enter or exit the banking system.

The majority of households that were banked in the previous 12 months and that experienced a significant income loss or a job loss did not become unbanked.[17] However, for households that did recently become unbanked, losing a job or experiencing a significant reduction in income appeared to be common triggers for bank account closure. Among households that recently became unbanked, 34.1 percent experienced a significant income loss or a job loss that they said contributed to the household becoming unbanked.[18] More than three-quarters of recently unbanked households that experienced a job or significant income loss said that those events contributed to them losing their accounts.

The majority of households that were unbanked in the previous 12 months and experienced a new job did not open a bank account.[19] However, among households that recently became banked, 26.6 percent reported a new job in the prior 12 months and 19.4 percent reported that a new job contributed to their opening a bank account. In other words, more than 70 percent of the recently banked households that reported a new job indicated that the change in employment contributed to their decision to open an account.

Table 3.3 Contribution Of Life Events To Bank Account Opening And Closing

For all households with non-missing recent bank status and non-missing life events, column percent

Life Event	Recently Unbanked		Recently Banked	
	Event Occurred	Event Occurred and Contributed to Account Closing	Event Occurred	Event Occurred and Contributed to Account Opening
Job or Significant income loss	44.9	34.1	37.2	12.9
Significant income loss	38.1	27.3	30.7	8.7
Significant increase in income	6.4	1.4	7.3	3.8
Job loss	35.4	27.6	23.0	8.9
New job	19.3	6.1	26.6	19.4
Retirement	2.0	0.3	2.9	1.5

---

[15] Among households that experienced a move in the last 12 months, about 44 percent also gained or lost a job and 35 percent also experienced significant income gain or loss.

[16] A multivariate model that included controls for household characteristics and the incidence of life events was estimated to identify the most important determinants of household exit and entry into the banking system. Among the various life events, job loss was the most important determinant of bank account exit, and a new job was the most important determinant of entry into the banking system.

---

[17] Among households that were banked and experienced an income or job loss within the previous year, less than 5 percent had become unbanked by the time of the survey.

[18] There was substantial overlap between the households that experienced job loss and those that experienced significant income loss. For example, among recently unbanked households that experienced a significant income loss, 75 percent also reported a job loss.

[19] Among households that were unbanked and got a new job in the previous year, less than 5 percent had become banked by the time of the survey.

Table 3.3 Contribution Of Life Events To Bank Account Opening And Closing

For all households with non-missing recent bank status and non-missing life events, column percent

Life Event	Recently Unbanked		Recently Banked	
	Event Occurred	Event Occurred and Contributed to Account Closing	Event Occurred	Event Occurred and Contributed to Account Opening
Significant increase in Household expenses	25.3	15.0	21.8	9.1
Significant decrease in Household expenses	5.7	2.5	4.5	1.0
Divorce or death	2.1	1.0	3.2	1.5
New marriage	2.4	0.5	2.5	1.5
Birth or adoption	6.3	2.2	3.7	1.2
Move or relocation	20.4	8.2	18.0	8.4

Reasons for Being Unbanked

As in previous years, all unbanked households were asked why they do not have a bank account although this question was revised in the 2013 survey, limiting comparability across years. In addition to a change in how the question was presented in the 2013 survey,[20] the list of reasons was changed; notably, the reason "do not need or want an account" was deleted to try to better understand why households feel they do not need an account. This reason was a popular response in both the 2011 and 2009 surveys.[21]

In 2013, the most common reason, selected by more than half of all unbanked households (57.5 percent), was that they did not feel they had enough money to keep in an account or to meet a minimum balance requirement. More than one in three unbanked households (35.6 percent) said that lack of money

was the main reason behind their decision to be unbanked. In 2011 and 2009, lack of money was also the most frequently selected reason for being unbanked.

The new life events questions provide additional context for households that reported not having enough money to have an account. About half (49.0 percent) of unbanked households that experienced a significant loss of income said their main reason for being unbanked was not having enough money. Among households with significant income loss that they said contributed to closing their account, 60.9 percent selected this as their main reason for being unbanked.

The second most common reason households cited for not having a bank account was a lack of trust in or dislike of dealing with banks: 34.2 percent reported this as one reason for being unbanked and 14.9 percent reported it as the main reason.

The third most common reason households identified for being unbanked was high or unpredictable account fees, cited by 30.8 percent of unbanked households as one reason and by 13.4 percent of unbanked households as the main reason.

Previously banked households were more likely (37.6 percent) to cite high or unpredictable account fees as a reason why they did not have an account than were households that never had an account (25.4 percent). Also, almost one in five (17.7 percent) previously banked households said that fees were the main reason why they were unbanked, compared to one in ten (9.8 percent) households that never had an account. Notably this is the largest difference between previously banked and never banked households regarding their reasons for being unbanked.

The new life events questions also lend additional context here: among households that became unbanked in the last year and had a significant loss of income that contributed to the bank account closure, almost one in five (18.0 percent) said that their main reason for being unbanked was that account fees were too high or unpredictable.

In 2013, households were asked, for the first time, whether they were unbanked because not having an account gave them more privacy for their personal finances. More than one in four unbanked households (26.4 percent) reported that this was one of the reasons why they choose not to have an account, but

---

[20] In the 2013 survey, respondents were able to indicate multiple reasons for why no one in the household had a bank account and then were asked to choose a single main reason from the indicated list. In 2011, respondents were asked only about the single main reason why no one in the household had a bank account. And in 2009, respondents were able to indicate all applicable reasons under three sub-categories (customer service, financial reasons, other reasons) and then were asked to select the main reason from the indicated list. As a result, the results from 2013 are not directly comparable to results from the previous surveys.

[21] In the 2011 survey, this was the second most frequently selected reason (selected by 21.0 percent of all unbanked households). In the 2009 survey, this was the fourth most commonly selected reason for never banked households (selected by 12.4 percent of never banked households) and the second most commonly selected reason for previously banked households (selected by 25.8 percent of previously banked households).

Figure 3.6 Reasons Households Were Unbanked

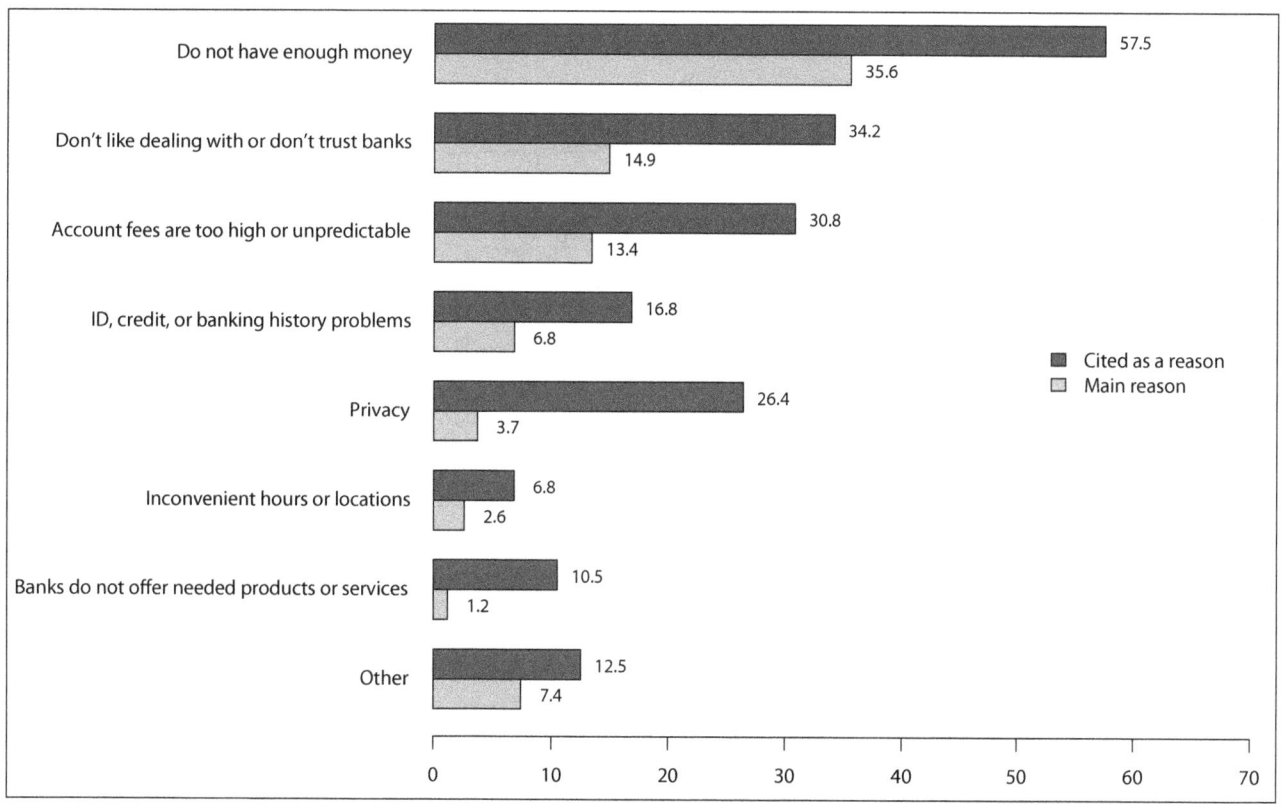

Figure 3.7 Reasons Previously Banked Households Were Unbanked

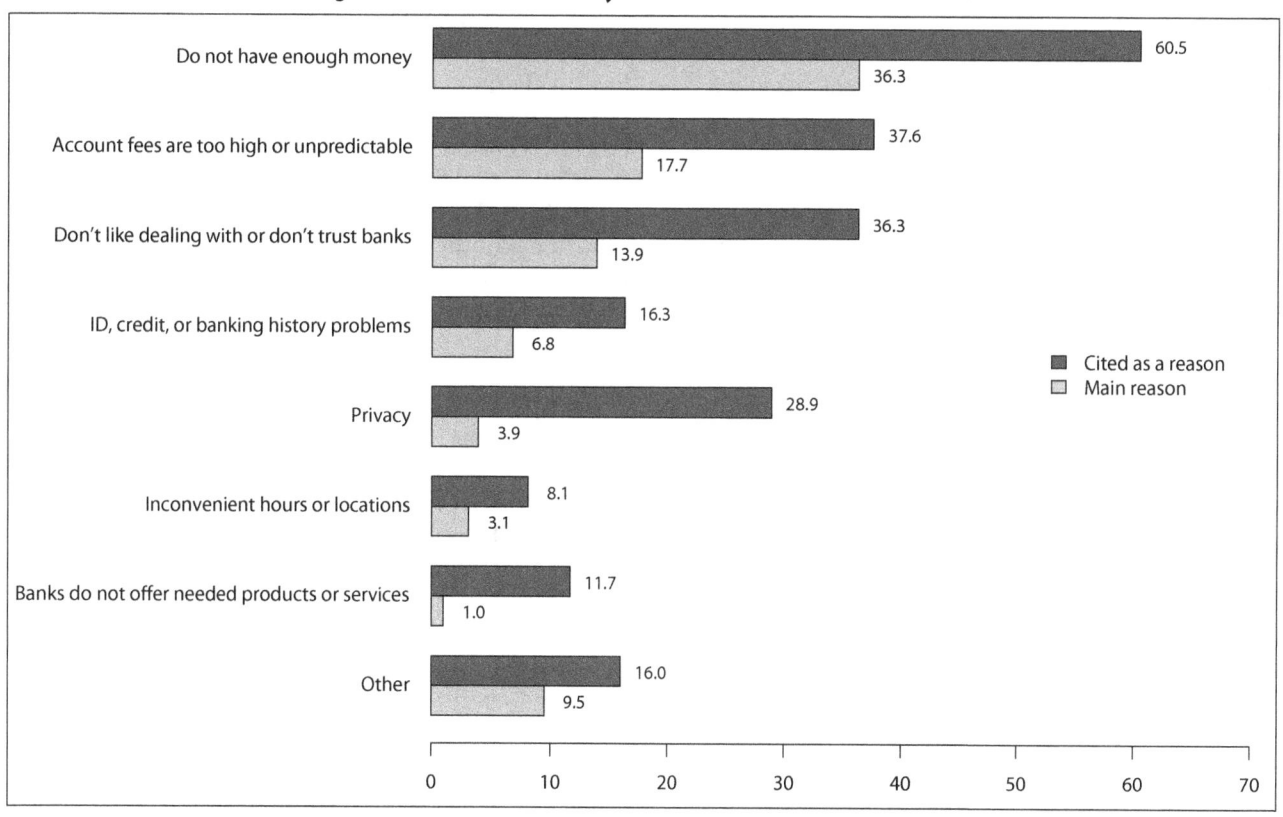

Figure 3.8 Reasons Never Banked Households Were Unbanked

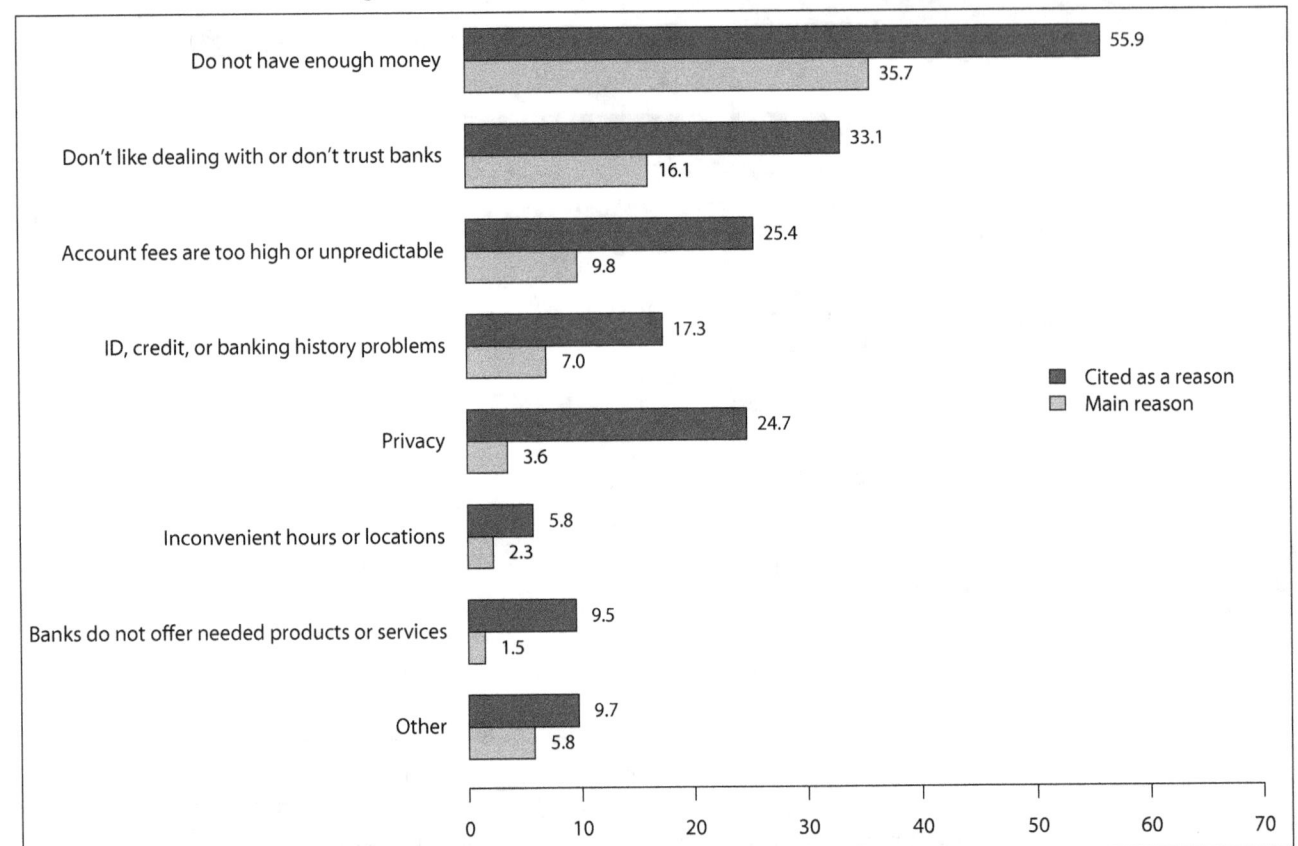

it was a main reason for being unbanked for just 3.7 percent of unbanked households.

A relatively small proportion of households (6.8 percent) were unbanked mainly because they could not open an account due to ID, credit or banking history problems. However, as in previous surveys, this reason is more important among unbanked Hispanic households, nearly one quarter (23.0 percent) of which said these problems were a reason why they were unbanked. About one in ten (10.7 percent) unbanked Hispanic households reported this to be the main reason they did not have an account.

Future Banking Plans of Unbanked Households

Unbanked households' intentions to join, or rejoin, the banking system provide additional insights into the banking status transitions discussed earlier in this section. The 2013 survey, like the previous surveys, asked unbanked households whether they intended to open a bank account in the future. Unlike the 2011 survey, which did not specify a time horizon for account opening, the 2013 survey asked households

how likely they were to open an account within the next 12 months. Most unbanked households (58.5 percent) reported that they were "not too likely" or "not likely at all" (not likely) to do so. Only about one-third (35.7 percent) of unbanked households reported that they were "very likely" or "somewhat likely" (likely) to open an account in the next 12 months, including 13.8 percent that reported being "very likely" to do so.[22]

Higher proportions of households that previously had an account reported being likely to open one in the next 12 months compared with households that had never been banked. Almost half (48.6 percent) of unbanked households that previously had an account reported being likely to open another in the next 12 months compared with only about one-quarter (25.2 percent) of households that had never been banked.

Recency of a household's banking relationship also appeared to be correlated with the household's reported likelihood of rejoining the banking system.

---

[22] In the 2011 survey, 60.7 percent of unbanked households reported not being likely to open an account in the future and 33.9 percent reported being likely to do so.

Almost three out of four (74.8 percent) unbanked households that recently had a bank account reported being likely to open another in the next 12 months, compared with 42.7 percent of unbanked households that had an account more than a year ago. These results suggest that many consumers who have had experience, especially recent experience, with a bank account find value in having one.

In addition, relatively large proportions of households headed by younger householders reported being likely to open an account in the next 12 months. See Appendix Table A-10 for households' reported likelihood of opening an account in the next 12 months by household characteristics.

Reasons that Recently Banked Households Opened Accounts

The 2009 and 2011 surveys provided insights into the reasons households were likely to open an account in the future. In both years, meeting transaction needs, security, and saving were consistently the most frequently reported reasons.[23] For example, in 2011 unbanked households that reported being likely to open an account in the future reported that their main reason for doing so were: "to be able to write checks and pay bills" (27.4 percent), "to put money in a safe place" (27.4 percent) and "to save money for the future" (23.8 percent). A smaller share of households (7.9 percent) selected "to take advantage of direct deposit of paychecks" as the main reason for wanting to open an account in the future. This is not surprising given that households are unlikely to be able to forecast future needs for direct deposit, which are dependent on current and future employers' payroll methods.

The 2013 survey did not ask unbanked households that reported being likely to open an account in the future why they wanted to do so. Instead, the survey asked recently banked households about the main reason why they had opened an account in the past 12 months. A majority of these recently banked households cited reasons related to meeting transaction needs: about one third (34.2 percent) opened an account "to receive direct deposits" and one quarter (25.0 percent) "to pay for everyday items, pay bills, and write checks". One in five (19.1 percent) recently banked households reported opening an account "to put money in a safe place" and roughly 7 percent (7.1 percent) selected savings as their main reason for opening an account.

Results from these surveys can inform efforts to increase the number of banked households. The 2013 results indicate that immediate, practical triggers, such as the need to receive direct deposits, can be important drivers in the decision to join the banking system. The 2011 and 2009 survey results show that longer-term goals such as savings are also important reasons that unbanked households want to open accounts in the future.

The fact that the largest share of recently banked households reported opening an account to receive direct deposits is consistent with the findings about the contribution of new jobs to account opening for recently banked households, discussed in the section on banking status transitions. A new job may offer new opportunities for the direct deposit of paychecks.

These findings suggest that promoting and encouraging direct deposit of paychecks could contribute to bringing unbanked consumers into the banking system. In addition, being mindful about the transaction, security and savings motivations that many unbanked households associate with bank accounts could help tailor products to meet these specific needs.

---

[23] In 2011, the survey asked households that reported being very likely and somewhat likely to open an account in the future about the reasons why they would do so. In 2009 the survey only asked about the reasons for opening an account to households that reported being very likely to do so in the future. Despite this difference in households that were asked the question, the most frequent reasons selected were similar in both years.

4. Checking and Savings Account Ownership, and Automatic Transfers

Checking and Savings Account Ownership

Consistent with 2011, checking account ownership in 2013 was considerably more widespread than ownership of savings accounts. The vast majority of all U.S. households (88.5 percent), including almost all banked households (96.1 percent), owned a checking account. Less than 70 percent (68.8 percent) of all households owned a savings account. Roughly two-thirds (66.8 percent) of all households owned both a checking and a savings account (see Appendix Table B-1).

In total, 29.5 percent of U.S. households (including the 7.7 percent of U.S. households that were unbanked) did not have a savings account, which suggests that opportunities continue to exist for banks to develop and implement innovative programs to facilitate household savings. Similar to the unbanked population overall, higher proportions of households that did not have savings accounts were black or Hispanic, foreign-born and unemployed compared with households with a savings account. Households without savings accounts were also more likely to have lower incomes and lower levels of education than households that owned savings accounts.

Among banked households, the underbanked were less likely than the fully banked to have a savings account. Slightly less than one-third (31.7 percent) of underbanked households did not have savings accounts compared with about one-fifth (21.2 percent) of fully banked households.

Recently banked households were less likely than those that had been banked longer term to have savings accounts. Almost half of recently banked households (47.2 percent) did not have a savings account, compared to less than one quarter (23.2 percent) of longer-term banked households.

Direct Deposits and Automatic Transfers into Bank Accounts

For the first time, the 2013 survey asked all banked households whether they had money directly deposited or automatically transferred into a bank account, including automatic transfers between accounts. The vast majority (80.3 percent) of banked households had money directly deposited into a bank account or automatically transferred funds between accounts. As noted previously, receiving direct deposits was the most frequent main reason for opening an account, given by about one-third of recently banked households. However, recently banked households were less likely to have direct deposit (66.4 percent) compared to households that have had an account for longer (82.1 percent).

Use of direct deposits or automatic transfers increased with income. Among households with incomes of less than $15,000, 71.2 percent used direct deposits or automatic transfers compared to 87.6 percent of households with incomes of at least $75,000. These differences could be partly due to differences in availability of direct deposit in different jobs.

Banked foreign born households (67.0 percent), particularly non-citizens (58.7 percent), were also considerably less likely than U.S.-born households (82.3 percent) to have direct deposits or automatic transfers to their bank account.

Among banked households that had direct deposits or automatic transfers, the vast majority (81.4 percent) deposited or transferred the funds into a checking account only. Fewer than one in five households (17.3 percent) that had automatic deposits or transfers deposited or transferred those funds into a savings account, including 13.2 percent who had money transferred into both a savings and a checking account.

Among households with savings accounts that had direct deposit or automatic transfers, 22.0 percent deposited or transferred funds into a savings account.

Figure 4.1 Direct Deposit And Automatic Transfer Bank Account Types For Households With Direct Deposit Or Automatic Transfers

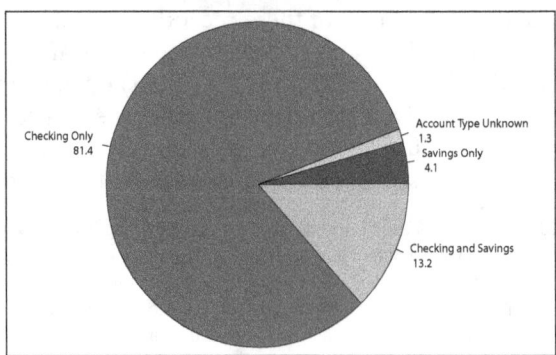

5. Prepaid Debit Cards

General purpose reloadable prepaid debit cards are a rapidly growing payment instrument that has traditionally been marketed with a focus on underserved households. Many, although not all, such cards store funds in accounts eligible for deposit insurance, and some of these cards are issued directly by banks to consumers. According to the 2013 Federal Reserve Payments Study, prepaid card payment transactions increased 15.8 percent annually between 2009 and 2012, reaching 9.2 billion transactions in 2012.[1] Similar to a checking account, these cards can be used to pay bills, withdraw cash at ATMs, make purchases, deposit checks, and receive direct deposits.

In 2013, 12.0 percent of all households had ever used prepaid cards. Their use was more common among unbanked and underbanked households. More than a quarter (27.1 percent) of unbanked households had ever used prepaid cards, compared with 19.6 percent of underbanked households and 8.8 percent of fully banked households.

Consistent with the growth in prepaid card transactions noted in the Federal Reserve Payments Study, the 12.0 percent of all households in 2013 that had ever used a prepaid card was higher than the 10.1 percent in 2011 and 9.9 percent in 2009.[2] Prepaid card use among unbanked households, in particular, increased substantially in this time: the share of unbanked households that had ever used a prepaid card increased to 27.1 percent in 2013 from 17.8 percent in 2011 and 12.2 percent in 2009.

Figure 5.1 Households That Had Ever Used Prepaid Cards By Banking Status And Year

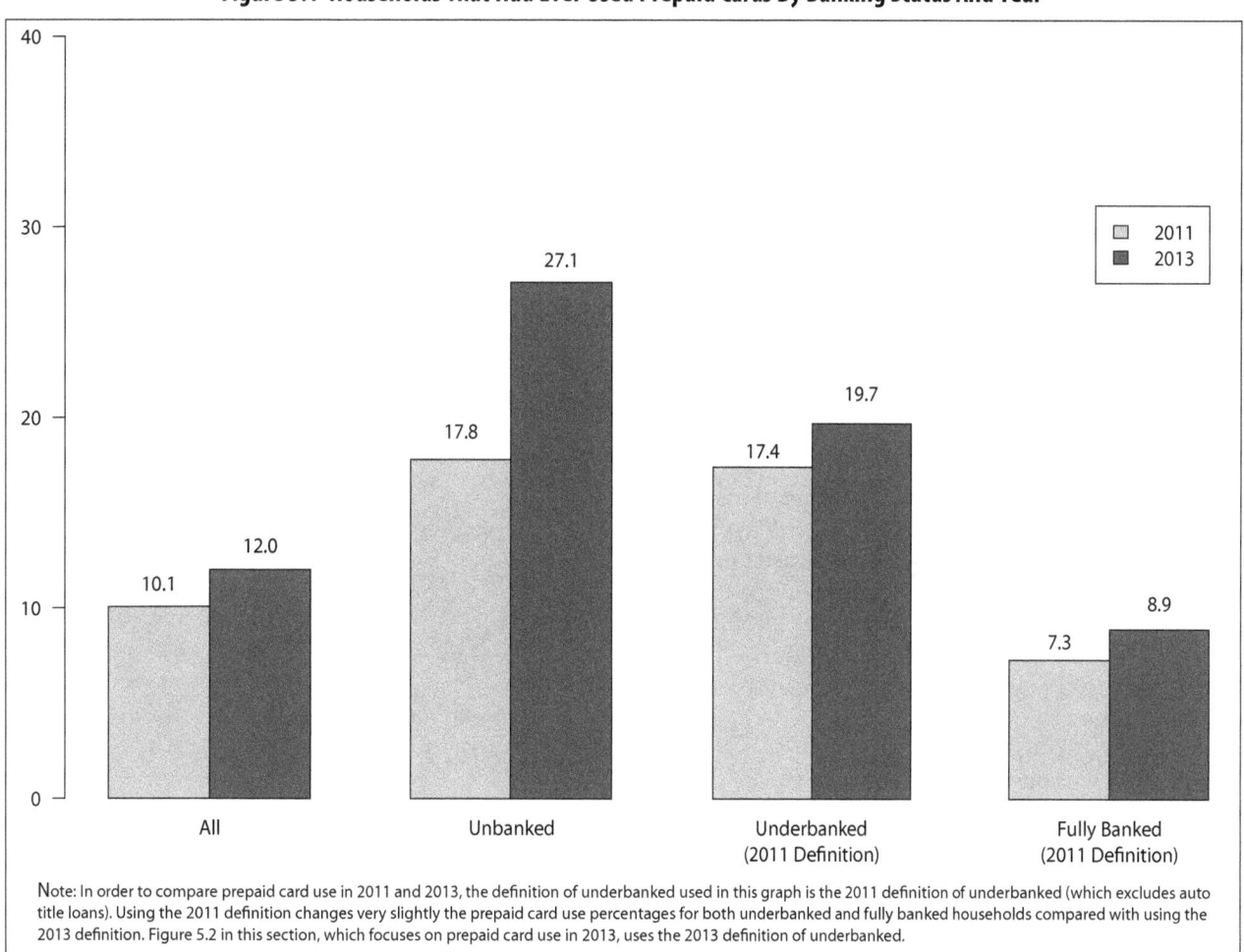

Note: In order to compare prepaid card use in 2011 and 2013, the definition of underbanked used in this graph is the 2011 definition of underbanked (which excludes auto title loans). Using the 2011 definition changes very slightly the prepaid card use percentages for both underbanked and fully banked households compared with using the 2013 definition. Figure 5.2 in this section, which focuses on prepaid card use in 2013, uses the 2013 definition of underbanked.

[1] Federal Reserve Board of Governors. 2014. The 2013 Federal Reserve Payment Study, Recent and Long-Term Trends in the United States: 2000-2012, July 2014. Available at http://www.frbservices.org/files/communications/pdf/general/2013_fed_res_paymt_study_detailed_rpt.pdf.

[2] The proportion of households with unknown prepaid card use increased to 5.7 percent in 2013 from 2.9 percent in 2011 and 2.2 percent in 2009.

Figure 5.2 Recency Of Prepaid Card Use By Banking Status, 2013

Legend:
- ■ Ever Used
- ■ Used in Last 12 Months
- ☐ Used in Last 30 Days

Category	Ever Used	Used in Last 12 Months	Used in Last 30 Days
All	12.0	7.9	3.9
Unbanked	27.1	22.3	16.8
Underbanked	19.6	13.1	6.6
Fully Banked	8.8	5.3	1.9

In the 2013 survey, we added new questions on households' use of prepaid cards, including use in the last 12 months and in the last 30 days. Nearly eight percent (7.9) of all households used prepaid cards in the last 12 months, and 3.9 percent had used them in the last 30 days.

The share of households that used prepaid cards in the prior twelve months and in the past 30 days varied substantially by banking status, as seen in Figure 5.2. Substantially higher shares of unbanked households had used prepaid cards in the last 12 months (22.3 percent) and in the last 30 days (16.8 percent) than the shares of either underbanked or fully banked households.

Unbanked and underbanked households made up the majority of prepaid card users. Among households that used prepaid cards in the last 12 months, more than half (55.0 percent) were unbanked or under-banked. Among households that used prepaid cards in the last 30 days, two-thirds (66.6 percent) were unbanked or underbanked.

For the remainder of this section, we focus on prepaid card use by households in the past 12 months which we refer to as prepaid card use.

Figure 5.3 Banking Status of Households That Used Prepaid Cards In The Last 12 Months

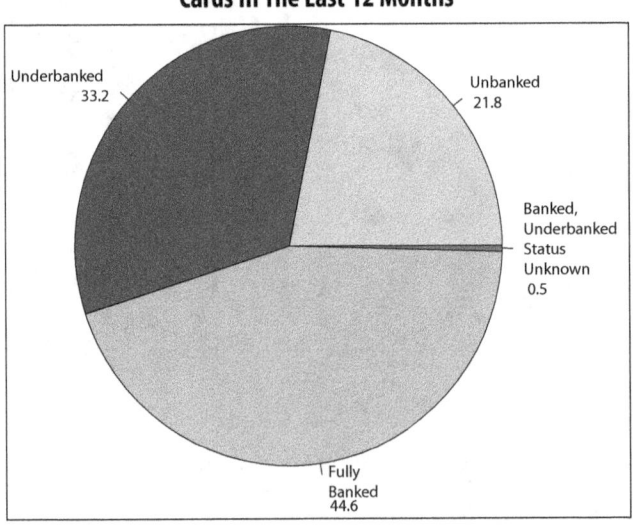

- Underbanked 33.2
- Unbanked 21.8
- Banked, Underbanked Status Unknown 0.5
- Fully Banked 44.6

Figure 5.4 Banking Status Of Households That Used Prepaid Cards In The Last 30 Days

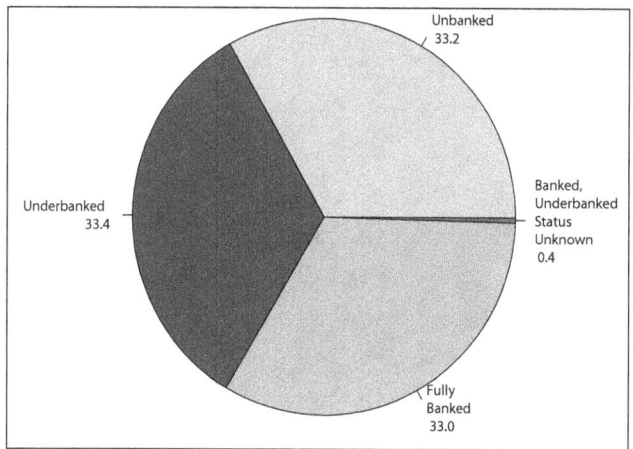

Unbanked 33.2

Banked, Underbanked Status Unknown 0.4

Fully Banked 33.0

Underbanked 33.4

Characteristics of Households That Used Prepaid Cards

Use of prepaid cards differed across households with different characteristics.[3] Younger households were more likely to use prepaid cards than older households. For example, 12.7 percent of households age 24 or younger had used prepaid cards compared with 3.0 percent of households age 65 or older. Other household types that were more likely to use prepaid cards include unmarried female-headed households (13.1 percent), the unemployed (14.8 percent), and non-home owners (11.6 percent).

Table 5.1 Prepaid Debit Card Use by Selected Household Characteristics, 2013

For all households, row percent

Household Characteristics	Used prepaid card in the last 12 months
All	7.9
Household Type	
Married couple	7.1
Unmarried female-headed family	13.1
Unmarried male-headed family	10.2
Female individual	6.3
Male individual	7.2
Other	7.2
Race/Ethnicity	
Black	11.5
Hispanic	7.8
Asian	4.5
American Indian/Alaskan	14.7

Table 5.1 Prepaid Debit Card Use by Selected Household Characteristics, 2013

For all households, row percent

Household Characteristics	Used prepaid card in the last 12 months
Hawaiian/Pacific Islander	9.8
White non-Black non-Hispanic	7.3
Other non-Black non-Hispanic	0.0
Nativity	
U.S.-born	8.3
Foreign born citizen	4.0
Foreign born non citizen	6.8
Age Group	
15 to 24 years	12.7
25 to 34 years	10.9
35 to 44 years	10.3
45 to 54 years	9.1
55 to 64 years	6.4
65 years or more	3.0
Disability Status	
Disabled	12.4
Not Disabled	8.7
Not Applicable	4.7
Education	
No high school degree	8.9
High school degree	8.1
Some college	8.8
College degree	6.7
Employment Status	
Employed	8.4
Unemployed	14.8
Not in labor force	6.2
Family Income	
Less than $15,000	11.4
Between $15,000 and $30,000	8.3
Between $30,000 and $50,000	8.3
Between $50,000 and $75,000	6.4
At Least $75,000	6.5
Homeownership	
Homeowner	5.9
Non-homeowner	11.6
Geographic Region	
Northeast	6.6
Midwest	8.9
South	8.4
West	7.1

---

[3] All reported differences are statistically significant in a multivariate regression model in which banking status was also included as an explanatory variable.

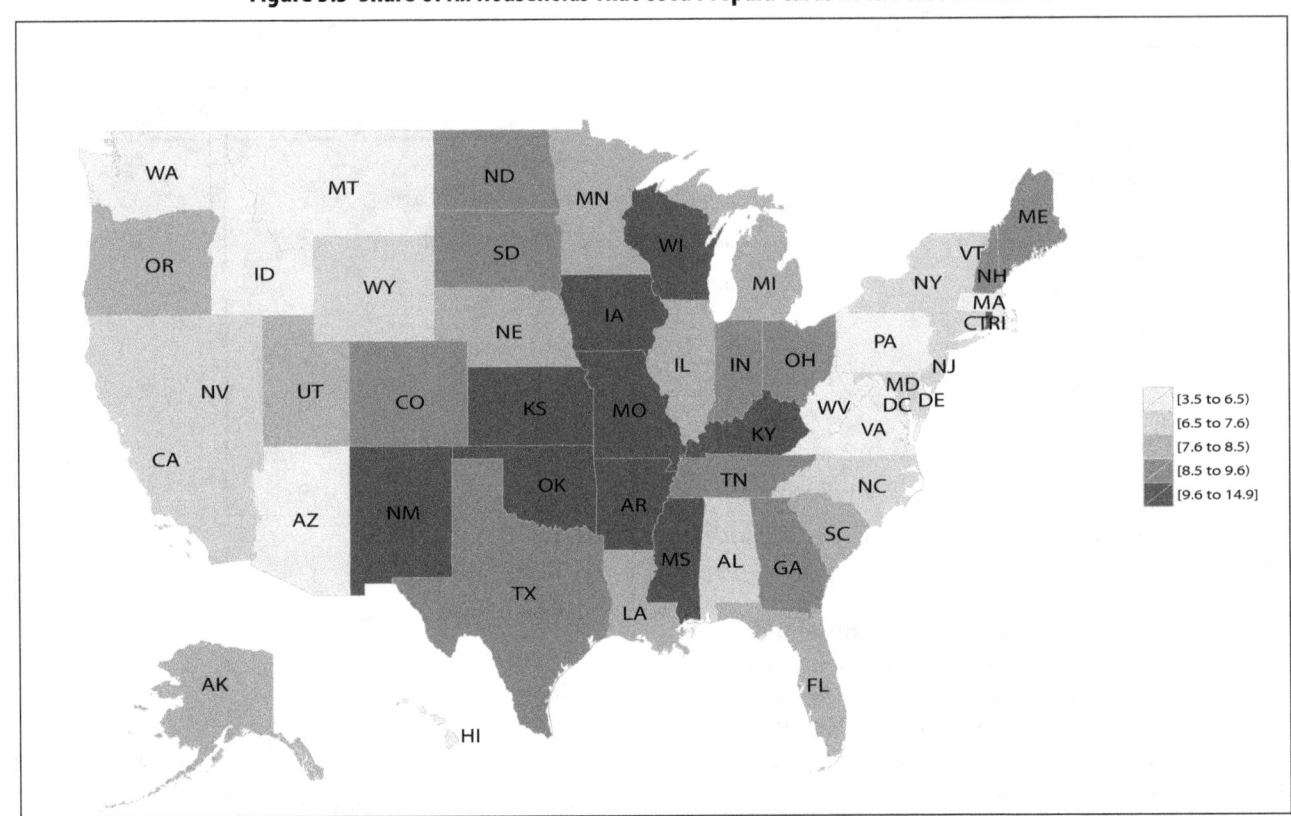

Prepaid card use varied somewhat among the four regions of the U.S., with a high of 8.9 percent of all households in the Midwest and a low of 6.6 percent in the Northeast. Prepaid card use also varied considerably by state. Hawaii had the lowest share of households (3.5 percent) that had used prepaid cards. The two states with the highest share of households that had used prepaid card were Mississippi (14.9 percent) and Oklahoma (12.9 percent).

Prepaid Card Use among Unbanked Households

As previously noted, unbanked households were significantly more likely than banked households – both underbanked and fully banked -- to have used prepaid cards. Even among unbanked households, there were some groups who were more likely to have used prepaid cards, such as households with some college (30.0 percent) and those with incomes between $30,000 and $50,000 per year (28.3 percent). In addition, previously banked households (33.0 percent) were almost two and a half times more likely than households that had never been banked (13.4 percent) to have used prepaid cards.

The Midwest had the highest rate of prepaid card use among unbanked households (26.7 percent) and the West had the lowest rate (17.9 percent). There was greater variation in prepaid card usage among unbanked households than among all households across different states. In three states, half or more of the unbanked households had used prepaid cards: Oregon (56.7 percent), Iowa (53.4 percent) and Minnesota (50.0 percent). And in three states, less than one in ten unbanked households had used prepaid cards: Arizona (9.4 percent), North Dakota (5.2 percent) and Montana (3.6 percent).

Reasons for Using Prepaid Cards

The vast majority of unbanked households that used prepaid cards appeared to use them to meet their financial transaction needs: the two overwhelmingly reported main reasons for using prepaid cards, cited by almost 8 in 10 (79.4 percent) of these households, were "to pay for every day purchases or bills" and "to receive payments". The third most frequently reported main reason for using a prepaid card was "to put money in a safe place", which was cited by 6.6 percent of unbanked households that used prepaid cards.

Household Characteristics	Used prepaid cards in the last 12 months
All	22.3
Household Type	
Married couple	20.6
Unmarried female-headed family	28.4
Unmarried male-headed family	18.7
Female individual	20.2
Male individual	18.7
Other	13.4
Race/Ethnicity	
Black	25.0
Hispanic	12.2
Asian	2.1
American Indian/Alaskan	28.4
Hawaiian/Pacific Islander	33.2
White non-Black non-Hispanic	28.2
Other non-Black non-Hispanic	0.0
Nativity	
U.S.-born	26.6
Foreign born citizen	6.0
Foreign born non citizen	9.1
Age Group	
15 to 24 years	21.1
25 to 34 years	25.7
35 to 44 years	24.9
45 to 54 years	25.0
55 to 64 years	18.7
65 years or more	8.9
Disability Status	
Disabled	27.9
Not Disabled	22.8
Not applicable	15.0
Education	
No high school degree	18.4
High school degree	22.4
Some college	30.0
College degree	17.3
Employment Status	
Employed	23.2
Unemployed	27.5
Not in labor force	19.8
Family Income	
Less than $15,000	20.9

Household Characteristics	Used prepaid cards in the last 12 months
Between $15,000 and $30,000	23.3
Between $30,000 and $50,000	28.3
Between $50,000 and $75,000	19.8
At Least $75,000	13.7
Homeownership	
Homeowner	16.1
Non-homeowner	24.0
Geographic Region	
Northeast	19.3
Midwest	26.7
South	23.6
West	17.9

While a majority (53.3 percent) of underbanked households that used prepaid cards also appeared to use them mainly to conduct financial transactions, there was more variation in the main reason that these households used prepaid cards. For example 12.3 percent reported using prepaid cards to send or give money.

Less than 2 in 5 (37.6 percent) fully banked households that used prepaid cards reported that the main reason they used prepaid cards was "to pay for every day purchases or bills" or "to receive payments", although that share was still high for households that had existing relationships with mainstream financial institutions. Almost one-third of fully banked households (31.5 percent) that use prepaid cards reported some other reason than the ones listed and about one in five of these households (20.7 percent) used prepaid cards to send or give money.

Use of Prepaid Cards and Alternative Financial Services

Households that used prepaid cards, whether banked or unbanked, were also more likely to have used an Alternative Financial Service (AFS) in the last 12 months compared to households that did not use prepaid cards.

Among unbanked households, those that used prepaid cards in the last 12 months were more likely (76.1 percent) to have also used a transaction AFS (check cashing, money orders and remittances) from

Figure 5.6 Share Of Unbanked Households That Used Prepaid Cards In The Last 12 Months

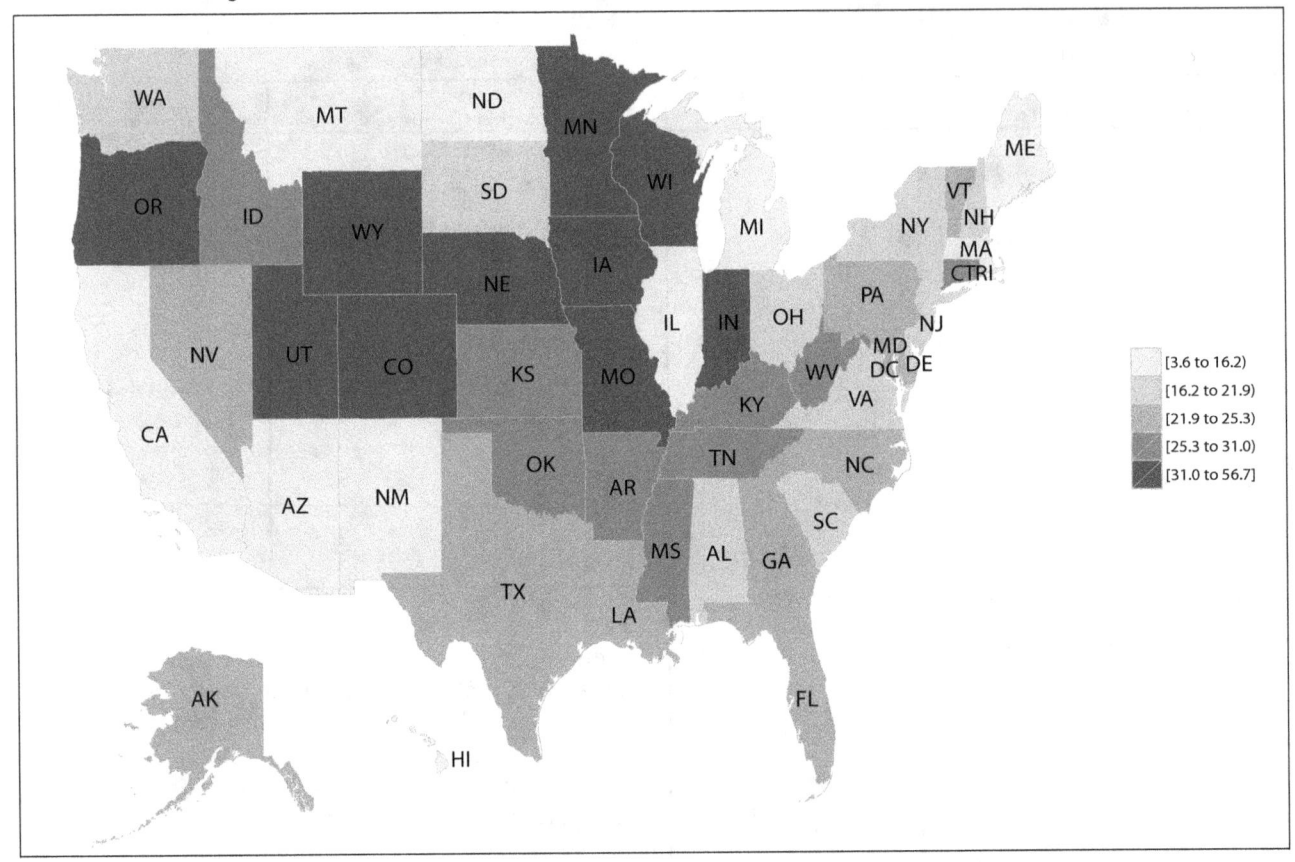

Legend:
- [3.6 to 16.2)
- [16.2 to 21.9)
- [21.9 to 25.3)
- [25.3 to 31.0)
- [31.0 to 56.7]

Figure 5.7 Main Reason Unbanked Households Used Prepaid Cards In The Last 12 Months

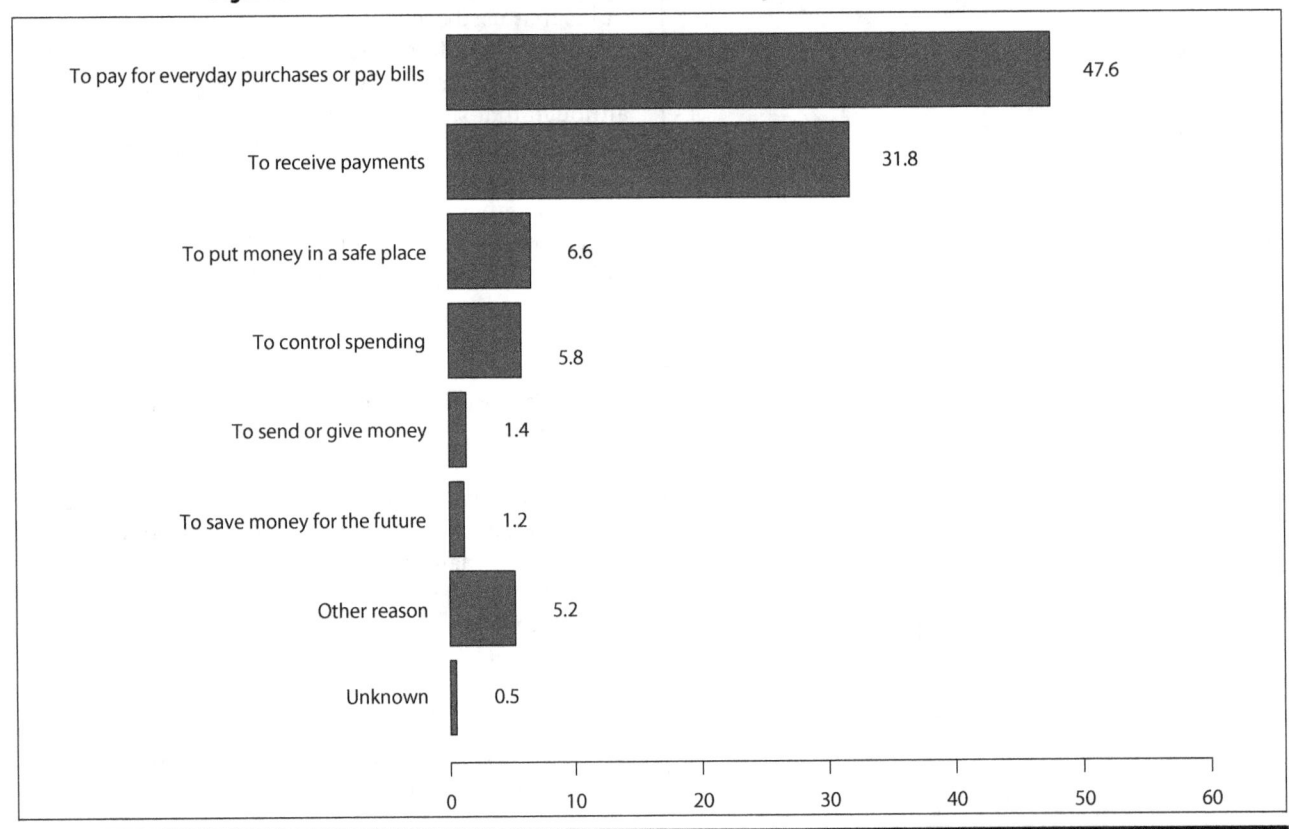

Reason	Value
To pay for everyday purchases or pay bills	47.6
To receive payments	31.8
To put money in a safe place	6.6
To control spending	5.8
To send or give money	1.4
To save money for the future	1.2
Other reason	5.2
Unknown	0.5

Figure 5.8 Main Reason Underbanked Households Used Prepaid Cards In The Last 12 Months

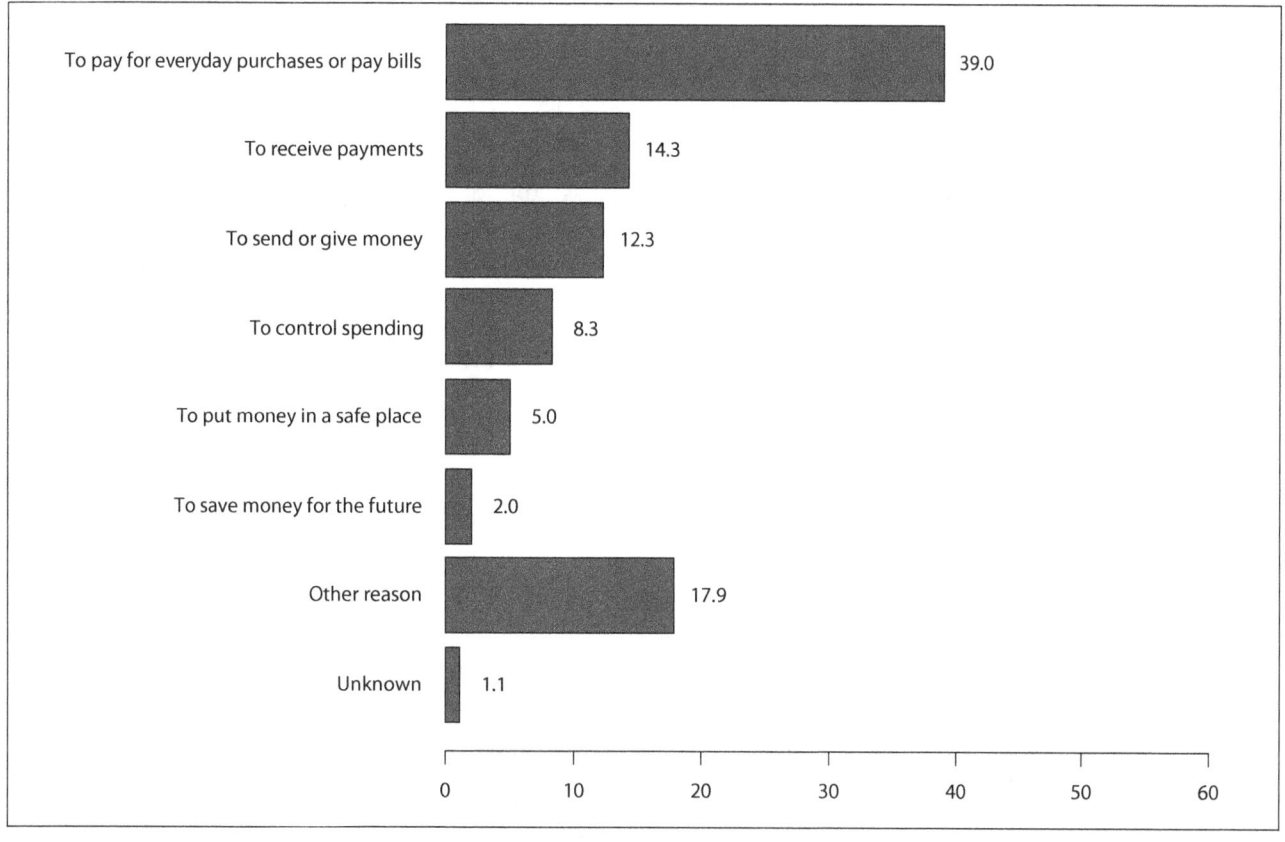

Figure 5.9 Main Reason Fully Banked Households Used Prepaid Cards In The Last 12 Months

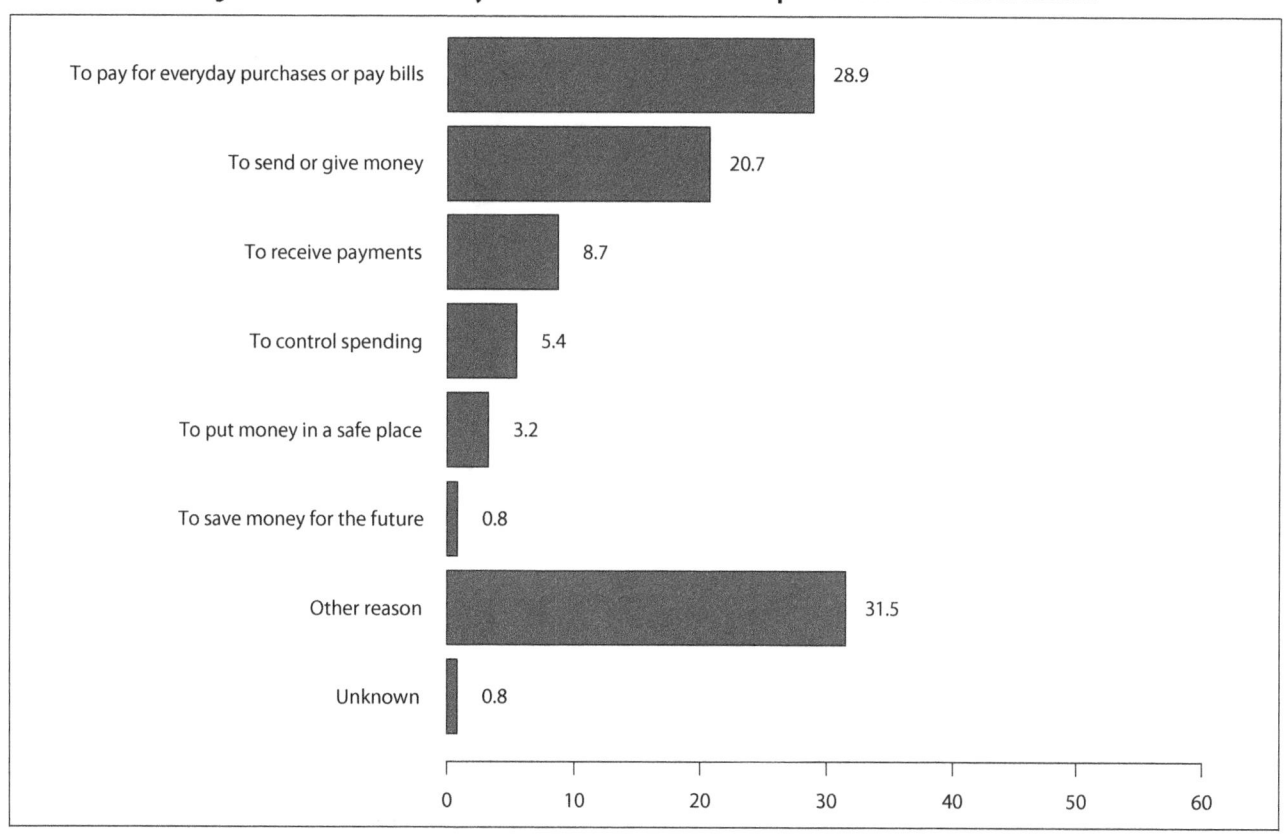

a non-bank in the last 12 months compared to households that did not use prepaid cards in the last 12 months (65.5 percent). Similarly, among unbanked households, almost one third (32.1 percent) of those that used prepaid cards in the last 12 months also used a credit AFS product in the last 12 months compared to 20.7 percent of those that had not used prepaid cards in the last 12 months.

The high rate of transaction AFS use among unbanked households that used prepaid cards suggests that these households had a variety of different financial transaction needs that they met using a combination of prepaid cards and AFS.

Sources of Prepaid Cards

Prepaid cards issued by banks could offer opportunities for prepaid card users to develop or sustain relationships with banks. In 2013, however, most households that used prepaid cards obtained those cards from entities other than banks. Nearly a third (31.5 percent) of households that used prepaid cards obtained them from large retail or department stores. Another 18.7 percent obtain them from grocery, liquor, convenience or drug stores. An additional 17.8 percent received their prepaid cards from someone else, and only 10.7 percent obtained their prepaid

cards from a bank branch. About four percent obtained them on-line.

Not surprisingly, the share of households that obtained their prepaid cards from a bank branch differed by banking status. Among households that used prepaid cards, 15.4 percent of fully banked households obtain their prepaid cards from a bank branch compared with 8.7 percent of underbanked households and 4.2 percent of unbanked households.

Among unbanked households that used prepaid cards, regardless of whether the household never had a bank account or held an account in the past year, approximately 4 to 5 percent obtained their prepaid cards from a bank branch. And those unbanked households that reported that they were very likely to open a bank account in the near future were no more likely to obtain a prepaid card from a bank than those that reported being very unlikely to open a bank account in the near future.

Overall, regardless of banking status, retail or department stores were the most frequent places from which households acquired the card: 34.2 percent of unbanked, 36.7 percent of underbanked, and 26.5 percent of fully banked households that used prepaid cards obtained them from these locations.

Figure 5.10 AFS Use in Last 12 Months By Banking Status and Prepaid Card Use in Last 12 Months

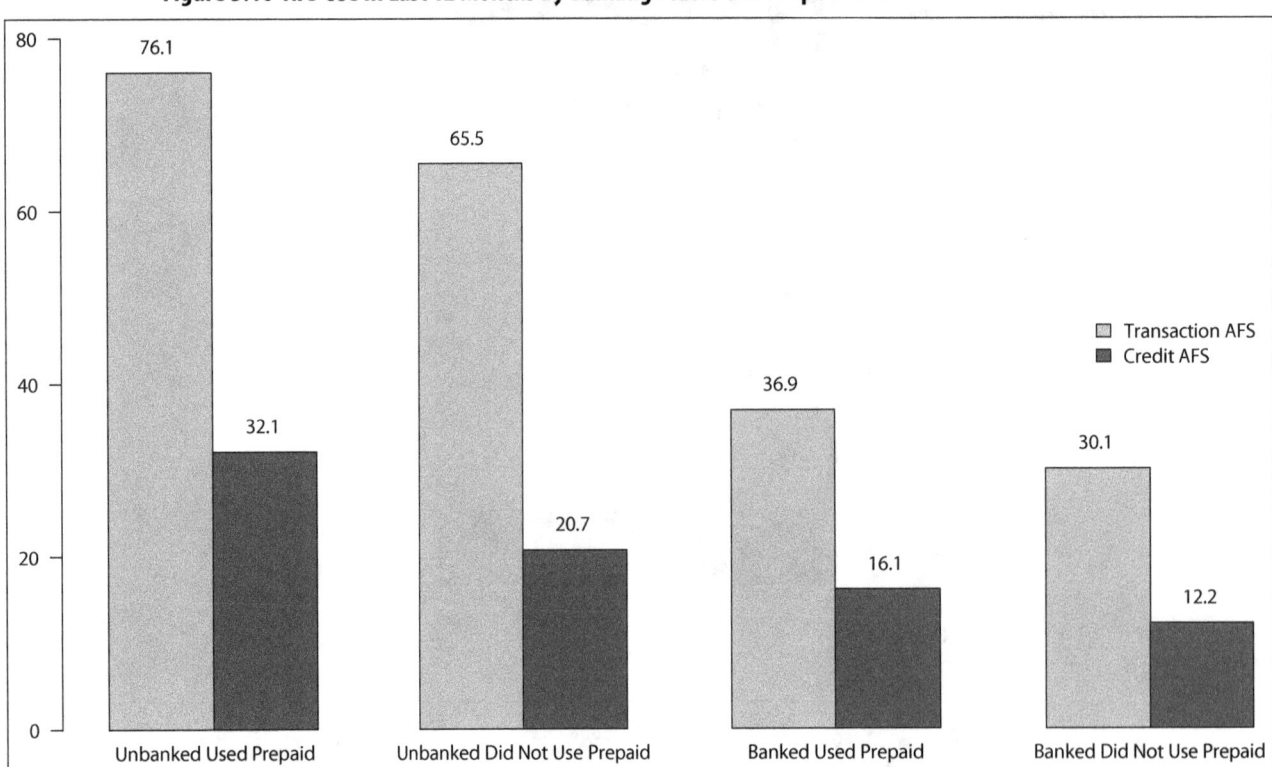

Figure 5.11 Sources of Prepaid Cards Of Unbanked Households

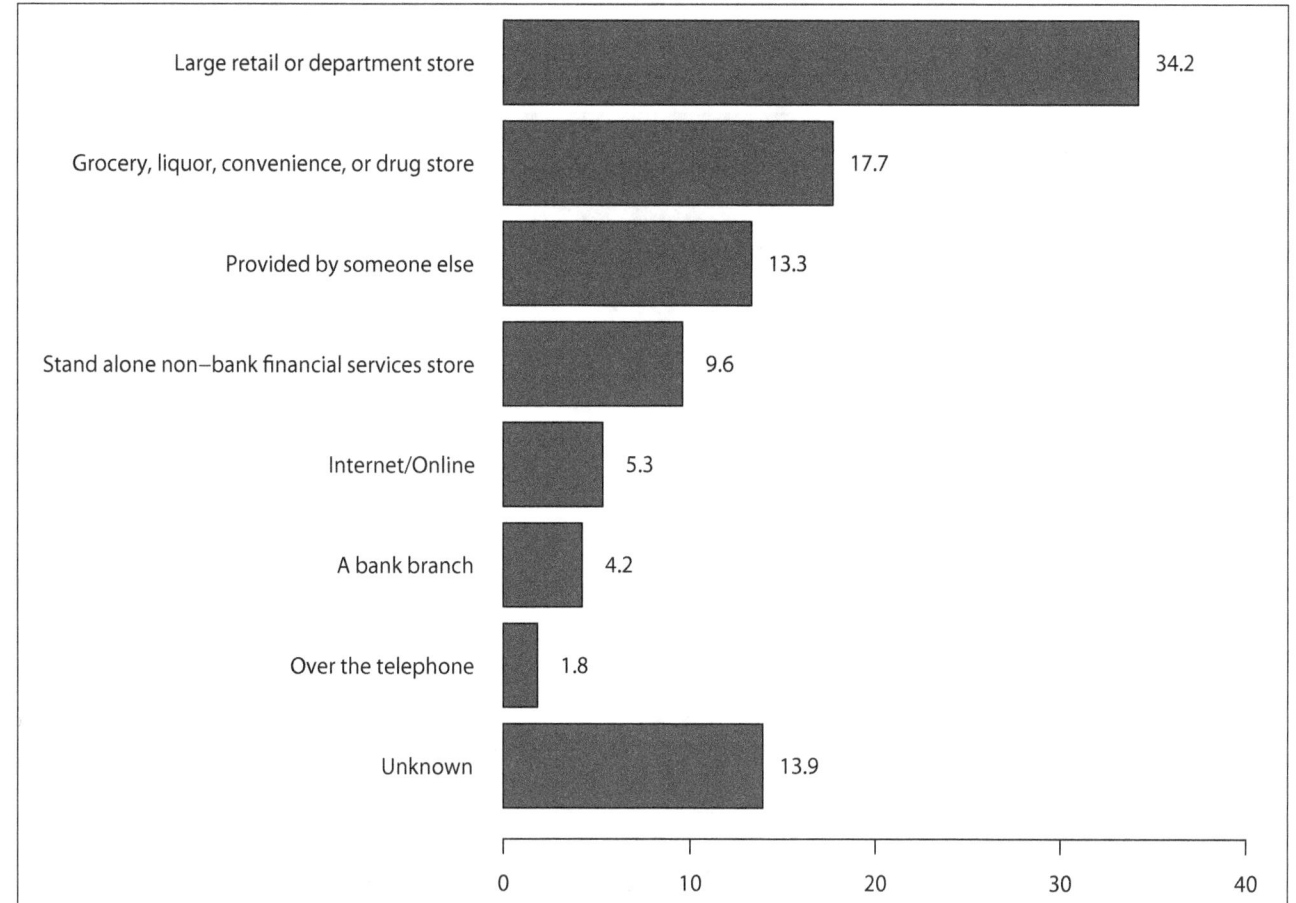

For unbanked and underbanked households that used prepaid cards, the second most common location for acquiring a prepaid card were grocery, liquor and convenience stores, which were used by 17.7 percent of unbanked and 20.2 percent of underbanked households. For fully banked households that used prepaid cards, the second most common source of the card was "provided by someone else" (22.1 percent).

Households that used prepaid cards differed by banking status in their propensity to obtain cards from stand-alone non-bank financial services stores: unbanked households were the most likely (9.6 percent), underbanked households were less likely (4.5 percent) and fully banked households were the least likely (1.1 percent) to obtain their cards from stand-alone non-bank financial services stores.

Reloading Prepaid Cards

Reloading of a prepaid card may indicate that the household is a more active user of prepaid cards than

households that did not reload their cards. Unbanked households that used prepaid cards were more likely (57.8 percent) to have reloaded their cards at least once in the last 12 months compared to underbanked (42.9 percent) or fully banked (23.4 percent) households that used prepaid cards.

Regardless of banking status, the most frequently used channel for reloading prepaid cards was retail clerk. Among households that reloaded their prepaid cards in the last 12 months, more than half (58.1 percent) of unbanked households, more than half (58.4 percent) of underbanked households and almost 1 in 3 (31.5 percent) fully banked households reloaded their cards using retail clerks.

The second most frequently used channel for reloading prepaid cards differed for fully banked and underbanked households compared with unbanked households. Among fully banked and underbanked households, the second most frequently used channel was bank tellers, used by 26.6 percent of fully banked households and 15.0 percent of underbanked households that reloaded their prepaid cards. Only 3.3

Figure 5.12 Sources Of Prepaid Cards Of Underbanked Households

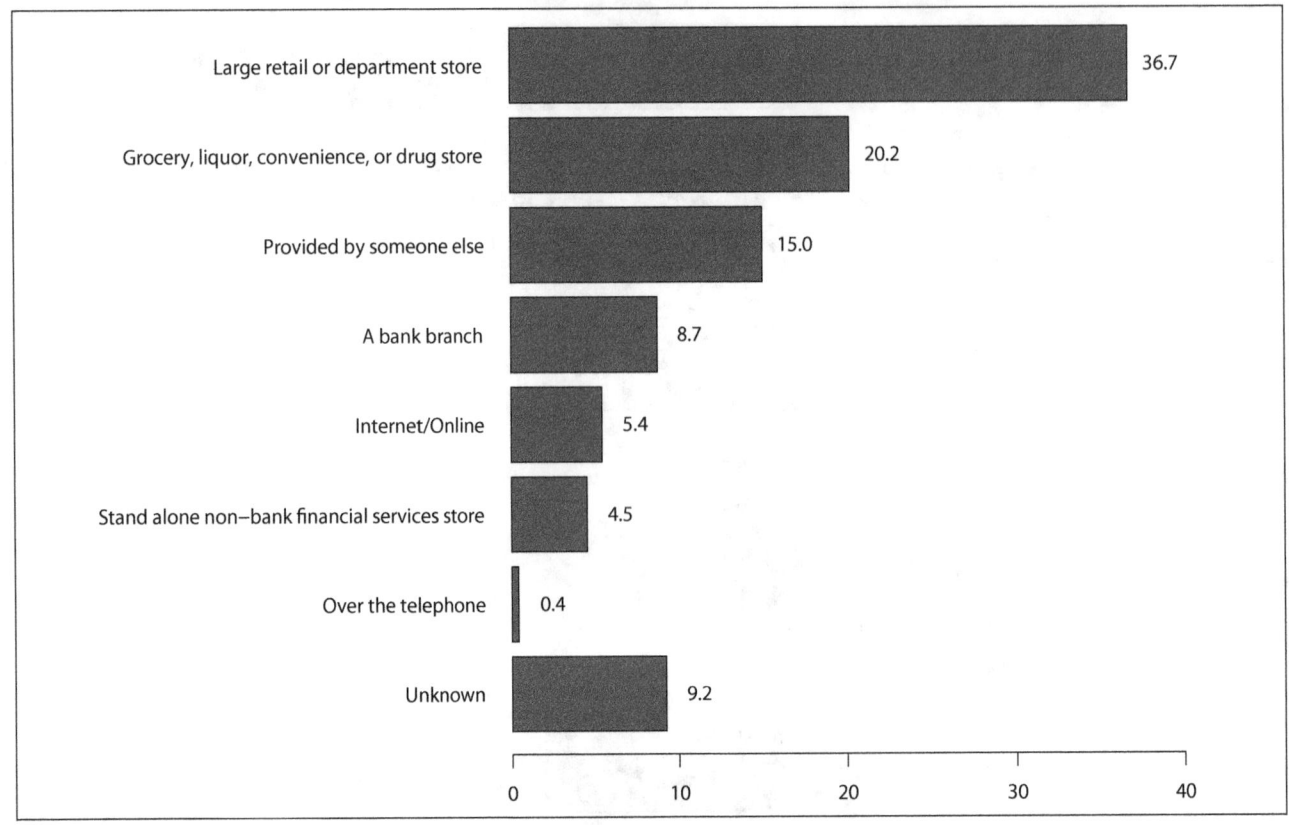

Figure 5.13 Sources Of Prepaid Cards Of Fully Banked Households

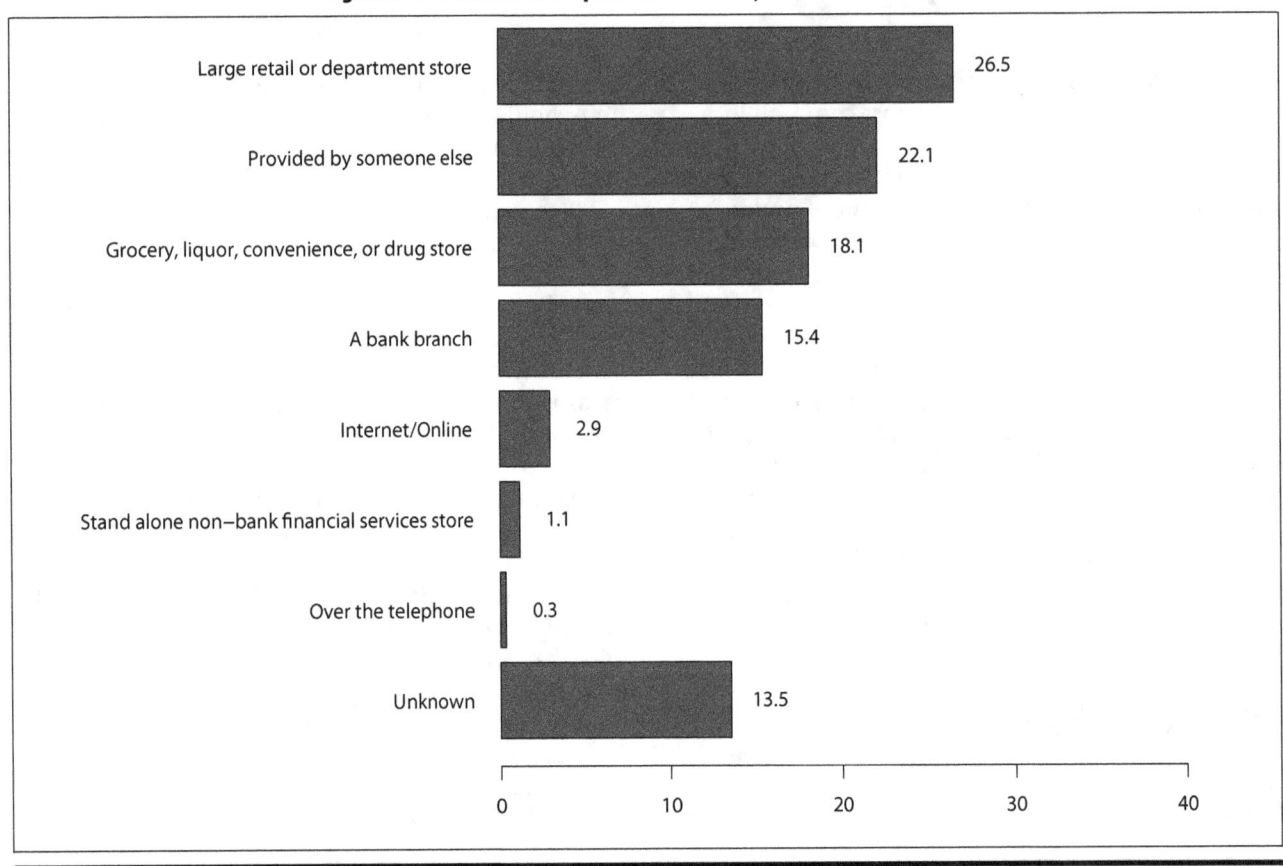

percent of unbanked households that reloaded their prepaid cards used tellers to do so.

For unbanked households that reloaded their prepaid cards, the second most frequently used channel was direct deposit, used by 27.7 percent of these households. Direct deposit was used by 12.9 percent of underbanked households and 12.5 percent of fully banked households that had reloaded their prepaid cards.

Banking History and Future Banking Plans of Unbanked Households that Used Prepaid Cards

Unbanked households that used prepaid cards were more likely to have once had a bank account and to want a bank account in the future compared with unbanked households that had not used prepaid cards. And previously banked households were more likely to have used prepaid cards than never banked households.

Among all unbanked households that used prepaid cards, 68.0 percent once had a bank account. In comparison, 38.5 percent of unbanked households

that had not used prepaid cards were previously banked.

Almost half (46.5 percent) of unbanked households that used prepaid cards reported being "very likely" or "somewhat likely" to open a bank account in the future, compared with 32.6 percent of unbanked households that had not used prepaid cards.

Reasons that Unbanked Households that Used Prepaid Cards Did Not Have an Account

The relative ranking of main reasons and reasons for not having an account reported by unbanked households that used prepaid cards were very similar to the reasons reported by unbanked households that did not use prepaid cards.

Almost 3 in 5 unbanked households, regardless of whether they used prepaid cards, reported not having enough money as one reason that they did not have a bank account: 59.5 percent of unbanked households that used prepaid cards and 59.7 percent of unbanked households that did not use prepaid cards selected this reason. And 32.0 percent of unbanked house-

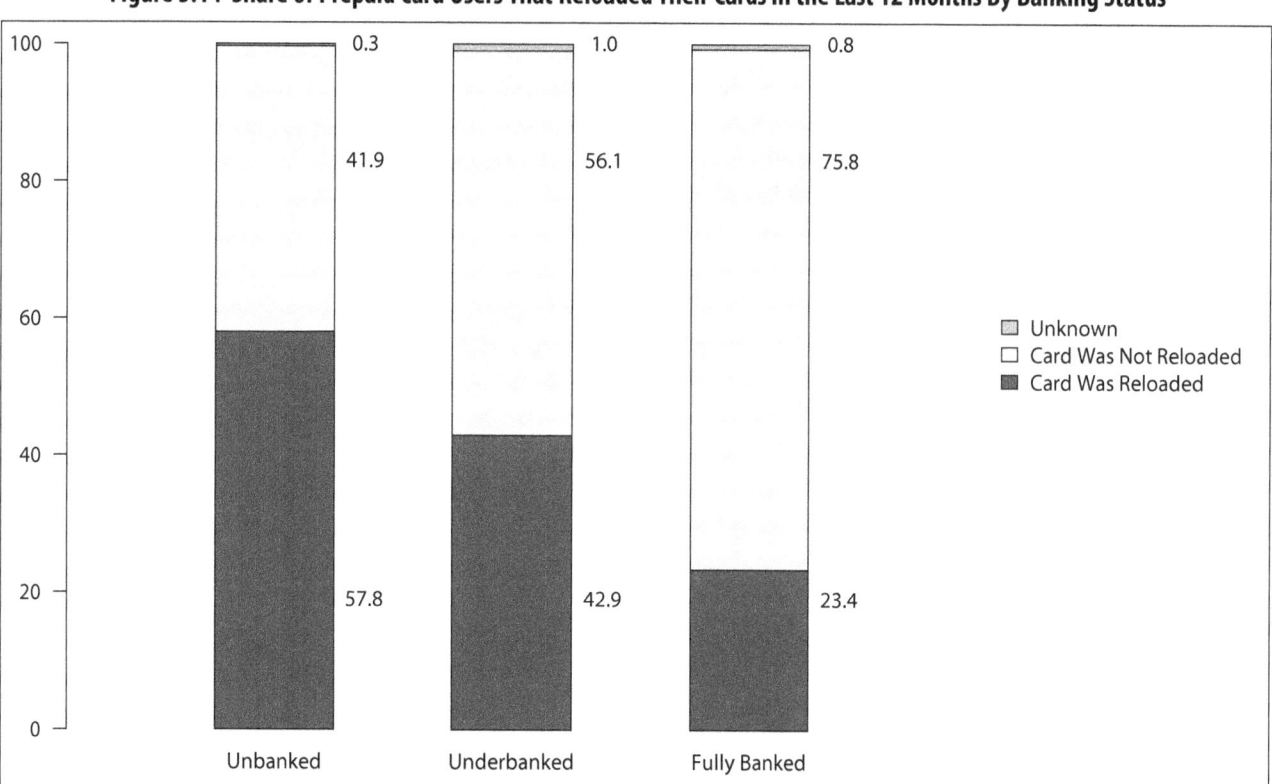

Figure 5.14 Share of Prepaid Card Users That Reloaded Their Cards in the Last 12 Months By Banking Status

holds that used prepaid cards reported this to be the main reason they did not have an account, compared with 38.9 percent of unbanked households that did not use prepaid cards.

The second most frequently reported reason, cited by 43.6 percent of unbanked households that used prepaid cards and by 32.8 percent of unbanked households that did not use prepaid cards, was not liking to deal with or not trusting banks. This was also the second most frequently cited main reason, reported by 18.0 percent of unbanked households that used prepaid cards and 14.7 percent of unbanked households that did not use prepaid cards.

Account fees being too high or unpredictable was reported by 40.1 percent of unbanked households that used prepaid cards as one reason they did not have an account, compared with 29.3 percent of unbanked households that did not use prepaid cards that cited this reason. This was also the third most frequently cited main reason, reported by 16.9 percent of unbanked households that used prepaid cards and 12.7 percent of unbanked households that did not use prepaid cards.

6. Alternative Financial Services

In the 2013 survey, questions on household use of AFS were revised, new questions were added, and some questions were dropped. Some of the new questions asked about household use of auto title loans, a form of short-term credit secured by a vehicle owned by the borrower and typically obtained by lower-income households. This change was implemented in response to feedback from external stakeholders and an understanding that auto title loans were used as frequently as other AFS credit products that had been included in previous surveys. In addition, new questions asked households that used transaction AFS where they obtained that AFS (such as the supermarket or a standalone AFS provider). Households were not asked why they used AFS providers instead of banks because this question was asked in 2009 and

12 months, and 12.0 percent of all households had used an AFS within the last 30 days.[1]

These results are consistent with previous survey results; however, they are not directly comparable because the types of AFS that were asked about differ across all three surveys. In 2011, 42.9 percent of households had ever used an AFS, and 25.4 percent of households had used one or more AFS in the last year, including 12.0 percent who had used an alternative financial service within the last 30 days.[2]

Transaction AFS continued to be more widely used than credit AFS.[3] In 2013, 21.9 percent of all households had used one or more transaction AFS in the

Figure 6.1 Recency Of Household AFS Use, 2013

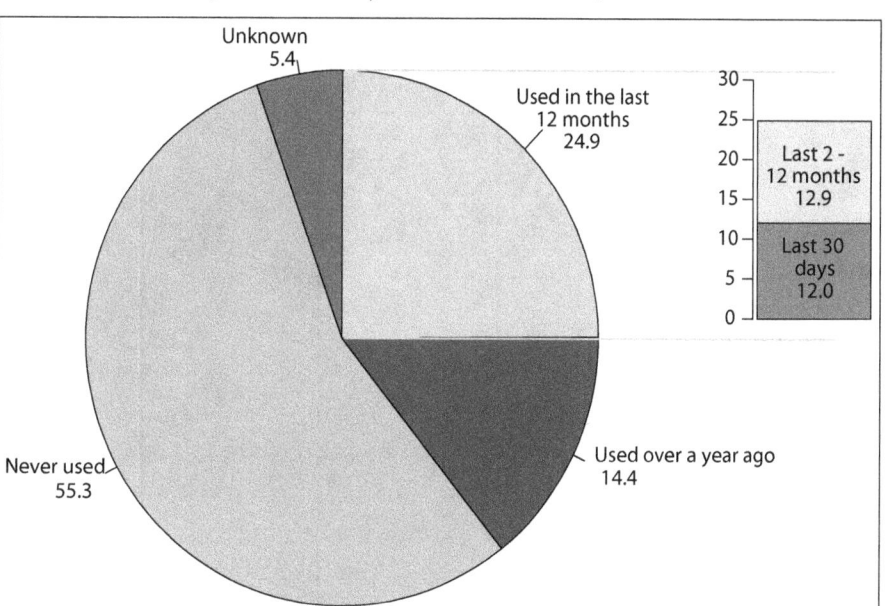

2011, and the answers were consistent across the two years. In addition, households were no longer asked how many times they used transaction AFS in the last 30 days.

In 2013, 39.3 percent of all U.S. households had ever used one or more of the following types of AFS: non-bank money orders, non-bank check cashing and non-bank remittances, payday loans, pawn shop, refund anticipation loans, rent-to-own services, and auto title loans. About one in four households (24.9 percent) used at least one of the AFS in the previous

---

[1] "Within the last 30 days" refers to whether the respondent had used one or more of the AFS products within 30 days of the survey month, June 2013. Such measures of "recent use" may be affected by seasonality of AFS use.

[2] The 2011 list of AFS did not include auto title loans, which are included in the 2013 list of AFS. Removing auto title loans to make the list of AFS comparable between 2011 and 2013, the proportion of households in 2013 that had used any AFS in the last 12 months would have been 24.7 percent, and 11.9 percent of all households would have used an AFS in the last 30 days.

[3] The transaction AFS included in the 2013 survey are non-bank money orders, non-bank check cashing, and non-bank remittances. The AFS credit products are payday loans, pawn shops, refund anticipation loans, rent-to-own services, and auto title loans.

last year, and 7.0 percent had used one or more AFS credit products in that time.[4]

Appendix Table D-1 AFS Use In Last 12 Months By Banking Status And Household Characteristics, 2013

For all households, row percent

Characteristics	Number of Households (1000s)	Percent of Households	Has Used (Percent)	Has Not Used (Percent)	Unknown (Percent)
All	123,750	100	24.9	69.3	5.8
Unbanked					
Unbanked	9,582	100	63.2	29.9	7.0
Has bank account	114,168	100	21.7	72.6	5.7
Household Type					
Married couple	59,102	100	20.1	74.7	5.2
Unmarried female-headed family	15,802	100	41.3	52.9	5.9
Unmarried male-headed family	6,327	100	37.5	57.3	5.2
Female individual	22,150	100	21.2	72.0	6.8
Male individual	20,240	100	26.2	67.1	6.7
Other	128	100	31.7	60.8	7.6
Race/Ethnicity					
Black	16,801	100	46.1	45.8	8.1
Hispanic	14,948	100	40.3	53.6	6.1
Asian	5,882	100	18.7	74.5	6.8
American Indian/Alaskan	1,464	100	38.6	56.5	5.0
Hawaiian/Pacific Islander	314	100	27.2	67.6	5.2
White non-Black non-Hispanic	84,310	100	18.1	76.6	5.3
Other non-Black non-Hispanic	NA	NA	NA	NA	NA
Spanish only language spoken					
Spanish is not the only language spoken	121,097	100	24.4	69.8	5.8
Spanish is only language spoken	2,654	100	46.3	48.2	5.5
Nativity					
U.S.-born	106,397	100	23.4	71.0	5.6
Foreign born citizen	9,252	100	26.9	65.9	7.1
Foreign born non citizen	8,102	100	42.8	50.3	6.9
Age Group					
15 to 24 years	6,244	100	41.5	53.5	5.0
25 to 34 years	20,464	100	33.6	61.2	5.2
35 to 44 years	21,408	100	29.6	65.0	5.4
45 to 54 years	24,551	100	26.7	67.6	5.7
55 to 64 years	22,710	100	20.9	73.6	5.4
65 years or more	28,372	100	13.1	79.8	7.1
Disability Status					
Disabled	10,841	100	38.7	55.3	6.0
Not Disabled	78,293	100	26.0	68.7	5.4
Not Applicable	34,616	100	18.2	75.1	6.7

[4] In comparison, in 2011, 23.3 percent of households had used one or more transaction AFS in the last 12 months. Considering only the types of credit AFS included in the 2011 survey, which did not include auto title loans, the proportion of households that had used a credit AFS in the last 12 months was 6.6 percent in 2013 compared with 6.0 percent in 2011.

Appendix Table D-1 AFS Use In Last 12 Months By Banking Status And Household Characteristics, 2013

For all households, row percent

Characteristics	Number of Households (1000s)	Percent of Households	Has Used (Percent)	Has Not Used (Percent)	Unknown (Percent)
Education					
No high school degree	13,871	100	39.5	54.4	6.2
High school degree	33,684	100	28.7	65.0	6.3
Some college	36,007	100	26.9	67.5	5.6
College degree	40,188	100	14.9	79.6	5.5
Employment Status					
Employed	75,587	100	25.6	69.1	5.3
Unemployed	5,436	100	41.0	54.2	4.8
Not in labor force	42,727	100	21.6	71.7	6.8
Family Income					
Less than $15,000	19,044	100	39.1	54.5	6.4
Between $15,000 and $30,000	21,763	100	33.1	60.5	6.4
Between $30,000 and $50,000	24,496	100	26.5	67.2	6.3
Between $50,000 and $75,000	22,552	100	20.9	73.6	5.4
At Least $75,000	35,895	100	13.8	81.2	5.0
Homeownership					
Homeowner	80,136	100	17.0	77.5	5.5
Non-homeowner	43,614	100	39.4	54.2	6.4
Geographic Region					
Northeast	22,199	100	23.6	70.4	6.0
Midwest	27,315	100	21.0	73.2	5.8
South	46,738	100	29.3	64.9	5.8
West	27,498	100	22.3	71.9	5.7
Metropolitan Status					
Metropolitan area - Principal City	34,510	100	29.6	64.1	6.3
Metropolitan area - Balance	51,229	100	21.2	72.7	6.0
Not in Metropolitan area	19,325	100	26.3	68.6	5.1
Not Identified	18,686	100	24.8	70.1	5.1

NA= Not available because the sample size was too small to produce a precise estimate.

-= For this table cell, the estimated proportion would round to zero. The population proportion, however, is likely to be slightly greater than zero.

Figures do not always reconcile to totals because of rounding.

Many households that used AFS used more than one type of product or service. Among all households, 8.0 percent used two or more types of AFS in the last year. Among AFS users, almost one-third (32.0 percent) used multiple products in the last year.

For the remainder of this section, we focus on the AFS included in the 2013 survey. We refer to households that have used AFS in the last 12 months as "AFS users." AFS usage in the last 12 months is referred to as "AFS use," while usage in the last 30 days is referred to as "recent AFS use."

AFS Use by Household Characteristics and Banking Status

The patterns of AFS use among households with different socioeconomic and demographic characteristics and with different banking statuses were very similar to results from previous surveys. AFS use was higher among younger, less educated, lower-income, and working-age disabled households. In addition, a higher proportion of unmarried female-headed family households and non-Asian minority households used AFS.

Figure 6.2 Household Use Of Transaction And Credit AFS In The Last 12 Months

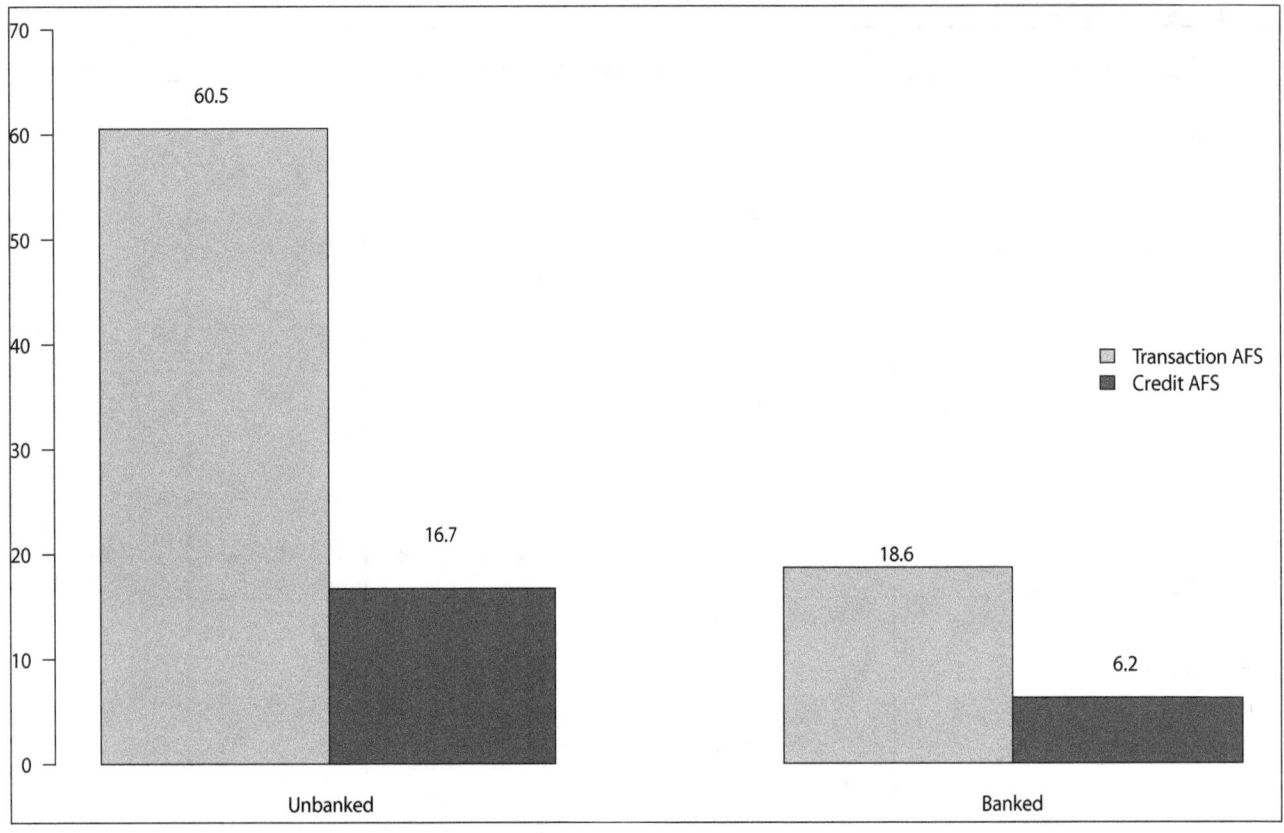

Figure 6.3 Household Use Of Transaction And Credit AFS In The Last 30 Days

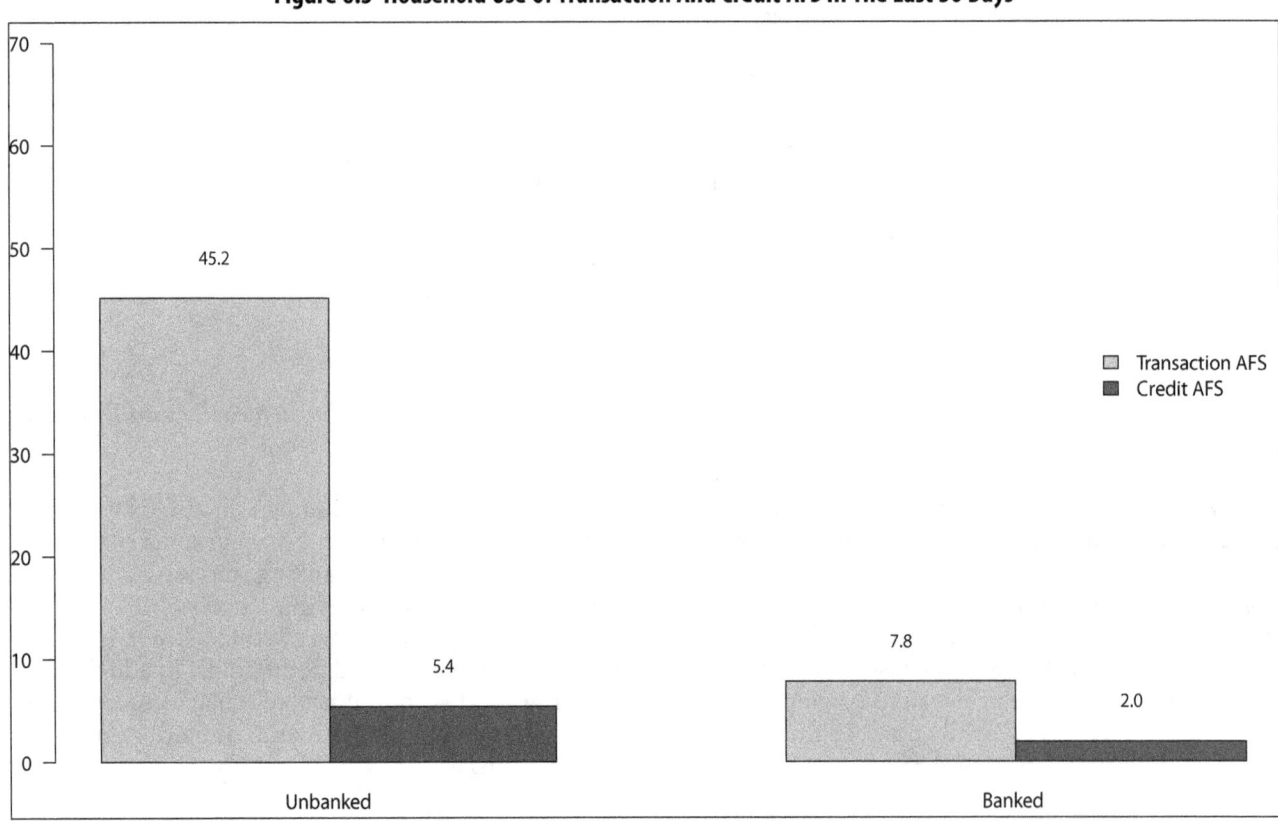

The rate of AFS use among unbanked households was high: almost two-thirds (63.2 percent) of them used an AFS. More than 1 in 5 (21.7 percent) households with bank accounts also used AFS. Both banked and unbanked households made more use of transaction AFS than credit.

Unbanked households were also more likely than banked households to have recently used an AFS. Almost half of unbanked households (47.0 percent) had recently used an AFS, compared with 9.1 percent of banked households. Notably, a much higher proportion of banked households that opened their account within the last year used AFS in the recent past (31.7 percent) compared to households that had been banked for more than a year (8.9 percent).

Figure 6.4 Use of AFS In Last 30 Days By Households That Used AFS In The Last 12 Months

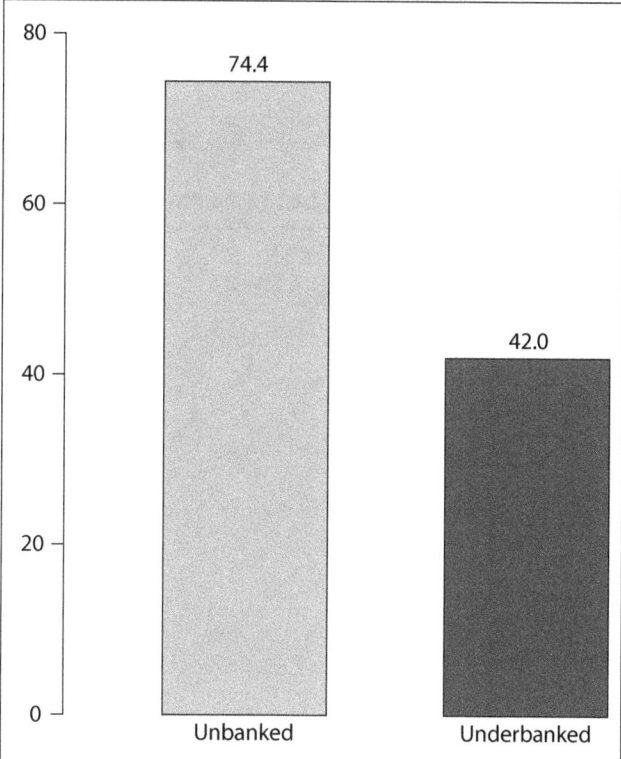

Among households that used an AFS, unbanked households were more likely to have used an AFS recently and to have used more than one AFS product compared to underbanked households.[5] This suggests that unbanked households that used an AFS may have been more active users of AFS than underbanked households. Specifically, 74.4 percent of unbanked households that used AFS in the last 12 months also recently used an AFS compared with

---
[5] Underbanked households are defined as households with bank accounts that also used at least one AFS in the last 12 months.

42.0 percent of underbanked households. And more than half (54.0 percent) of unbanked households that used AFS used multiple AFS products compared with about one in four (26.6 percent) underbanked households.

Figure 6.5 Count Of AFS Types For Households That Used AFS In The Last 12 Months

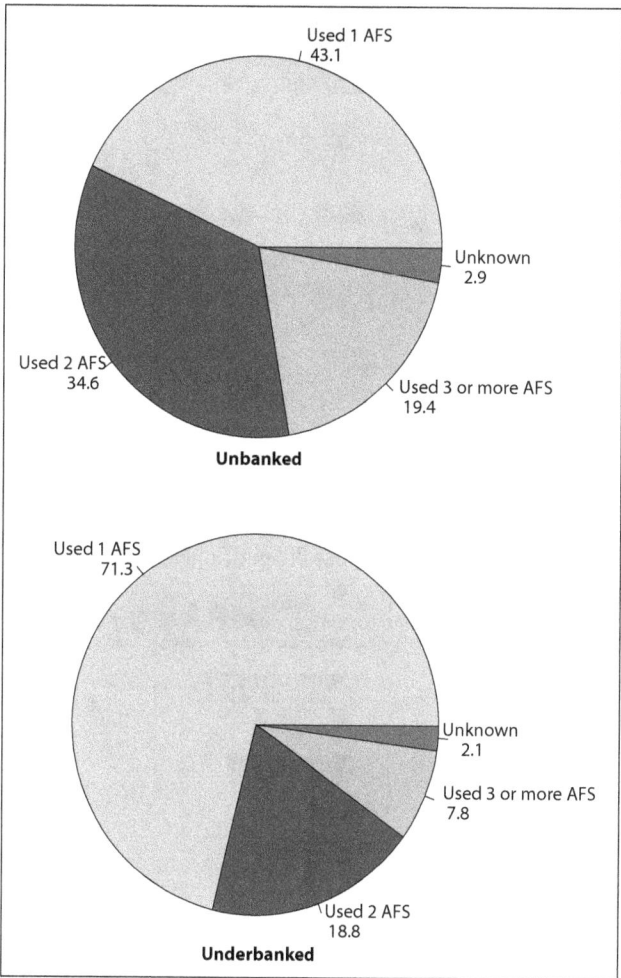

Use of Transaction AFS Products

Consistent with findings from the previous surveys, money orders were the most commonly used AFS, which were used by 17.3 percent of all households. The other transaction AFS were used by smaller proportions of households: 6.5 percent of all households used non-bank check cashing, and 3.7 percent used remittances.

Unbanked households appeared to be active users of transaction AFS, especially of money orders and check cashing. For example, 60.5 percent of unbanked households had used a transaction AFS and 45.2 percent had done so recently. Among

Figure 6.6 Use Of Specific AFS By Unbanked Households That Used AFS In The Last 12 Months

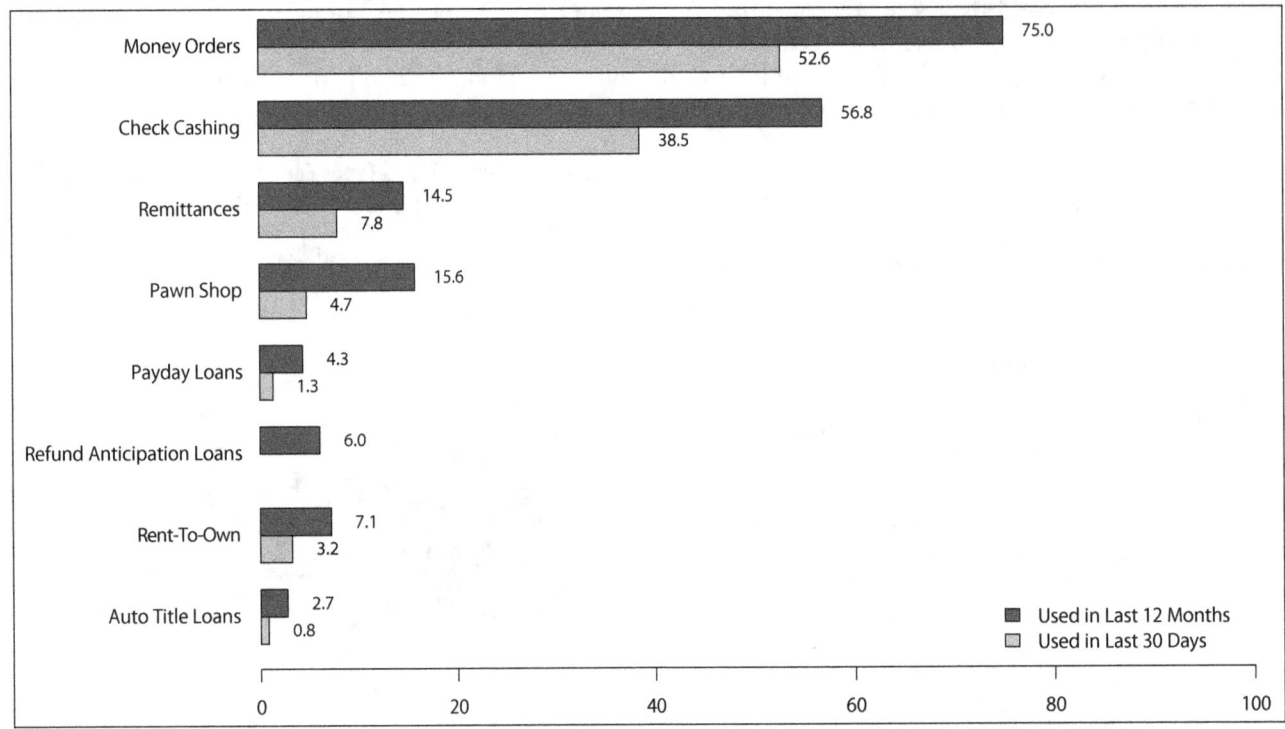

Figure 6.7 Use Of Specific AFS By Underbanked Households That Used AFS In The Last 12 Months

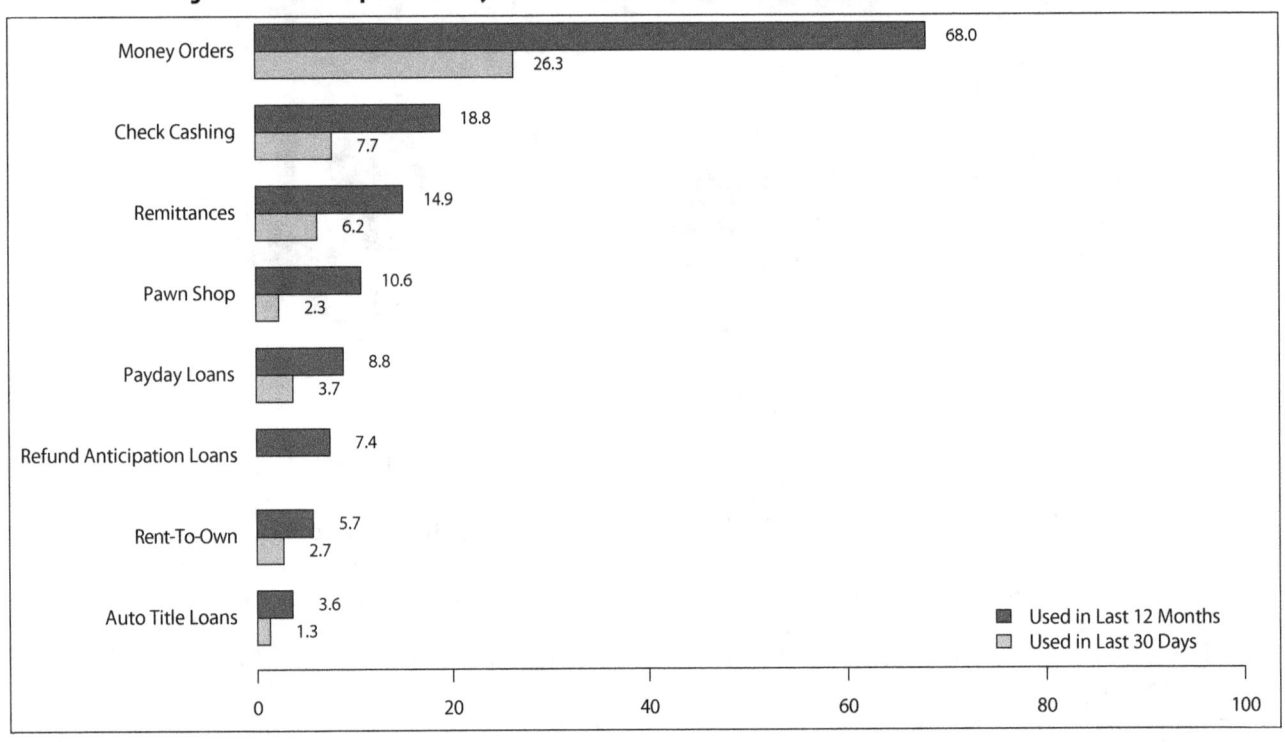

unbanked households that had used an AFS (either transaction or credit), more than 3 out of 4 (75.0 percent) had obtained a non-bank money order and more than half (52.6 percent) had done so recently. Also, among unbanked households that had used an AFS, more than half (56.8 percent) had cashed a check at a non-bank location and more than 1 in 3 (38.5 percent) had done so in the last 30 days. The high proportions of unbanked households that used non-bank check cashing and non-bank money orders in the last 12 months and in the last 30 days suggests that some unbanked households were using these transaction AFS products as substitutes for the transactions functions provided by a checking account.

Underbanked households also frequently used non-bank money orders (68.0 percent) although only about 1 in 4 (26.3 percent) did so recently. Even fewer underbanked households used non-bank check cashing (18.8 percent) and fewer than 1 in 10 (7.7 percent) did so recently.

Use of Credit AFS Products

AFS credit products were less commonly used than transaction AFS, consistent with previous survey findings: 7.0 percent of all households used at least one type of AFS credit product. Auto title loans, which were asked about for the first time in 2013, were used by less than 1 percent (0.9 percent) of households in the last year. The results for other AFS credit products were consistent with results from 2011. Two percent of all households used payday loans, 2.9 percent used pawn shops, 1.5 percent used rent-to-own stores, and 1.8 percent used refund anticipation loans.

The relatively low use of credit AFS among both unbanked and underbanked households may be due to the nature of the products and the fact that transaction needs are often regular and recurring, while credit needs, or the opportunities to obtain credit, may not occur as frequently.

Relatively small shares of unbanked households used pawn shops (9.9 percent), rent-to-own services (4.5 percent), refund anticipation loans (3.8 percent), and auto title loans (1.7 percent). Also, only 2.7 percent of unbanked households used payday loans, which generally require the borrower to have a bank account, in the past 12 months.[6] Among unbanked households that used at least one AFS in the last 12

months, use of AFS credit products was somewhat higher: 15.6 percent used pawn shops, 7.1 percent used rent-to-own services, 6.0 percent used refund anticipation loans, 2.7 percent used auto title loans and 4.3 percent used payday loans in the last 12 months.

Among underbanked households, 10.6 percent used pawn shops, 8.8 percent used payday loans, 7.4 percent used refund anticipation loans, 5.7 percent used rent-to-own services, and 3.6 percent used auto title loans.

Locations From Which Households Obtained AFS Products

The 2013 results provide new insights about where households obtained the AFS that they used. Grocery, liquor, convenience and drug stores were the most common locations from which households obtained transaction AFS, although relatively large proportions also obtained these services at large retail/department stores (such as Walmart or Kmart). Specifically, 37.8 percent of households that used non-bank check cashing did so at a grocery, liquor, convenience or drugstore, while 31.4 percent used a large retail or department store and 24.3 percent cashed checks at a stand-alone non-bank financial services provider.

Grocery, liquor, convenience and drug stores were also the most common non-bank locations from which households purchased money orders: 37.8 percent of households that used non-bank money orders bought them at such stores. Another 29.7 percent purchased their money orders from the post office.

Almost one-third (32.9 percent) of households that used non-bank remittances most commonly obtained them from grocery, liquor, convenience and drug stores, 19.0 percent from retail/department stores, and 26.3 percent from standalone AFS providers.[7] Very small proportions of households that used non-bank remittances most commonly accessed these services via a mobile phone (1.2 percent) or online using a computer (6.9 percent).

Relative to underbanked households, larger proportions of unbanked households that used AFS obtained their transaction AFS products from stand-alone AFS providers. Specifically, 29.3 percent of

---

[6] Among previously banked households, about 3.5 percent reported receiving a payday loan within the last 12 months.

[7] The proportion of remittance users who responded that they got their remittances from somewhere other than the choices provided, or did not know where they were obtained, was relatively high, at 13.7 percent.

Figure 6.8 Non-Bank Locations Used By Households To Cash Checks In The Last 12 Months

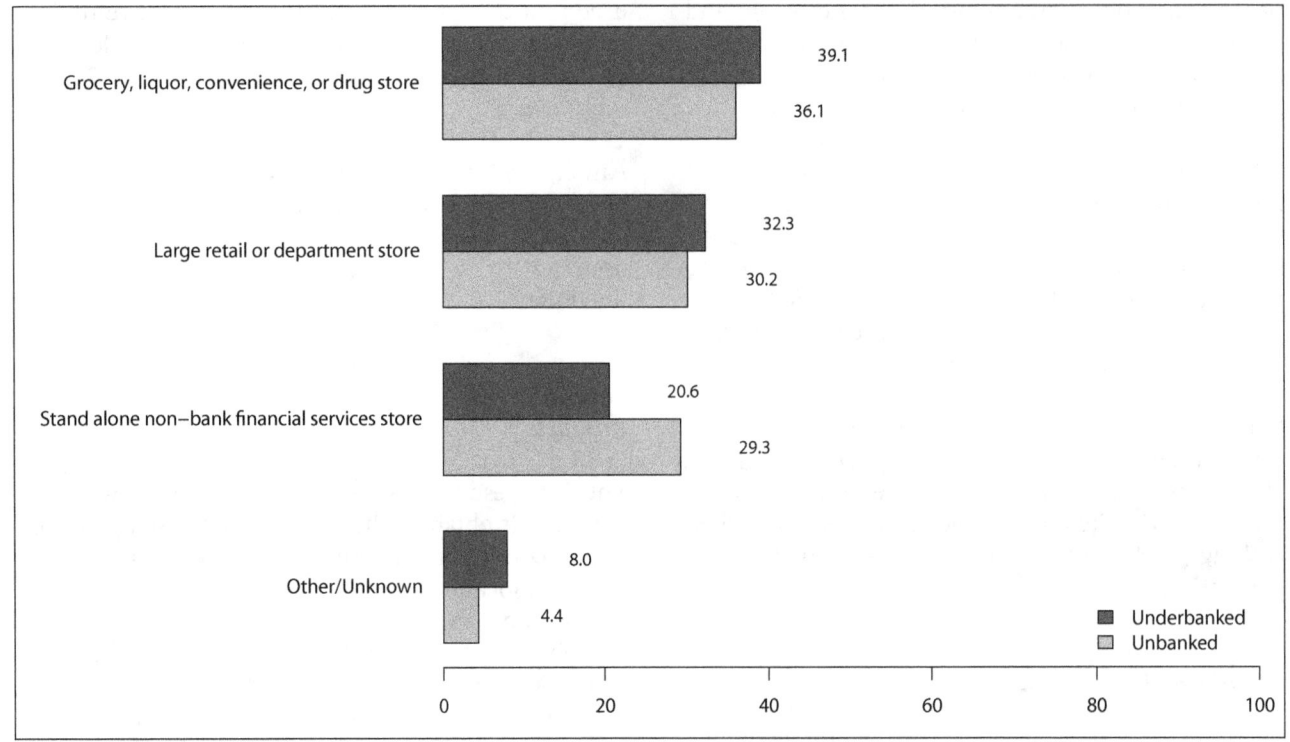

Figure 6.9 Non-Bank Locations Used By Households To Obtain Money Orders In The Last 12 Months

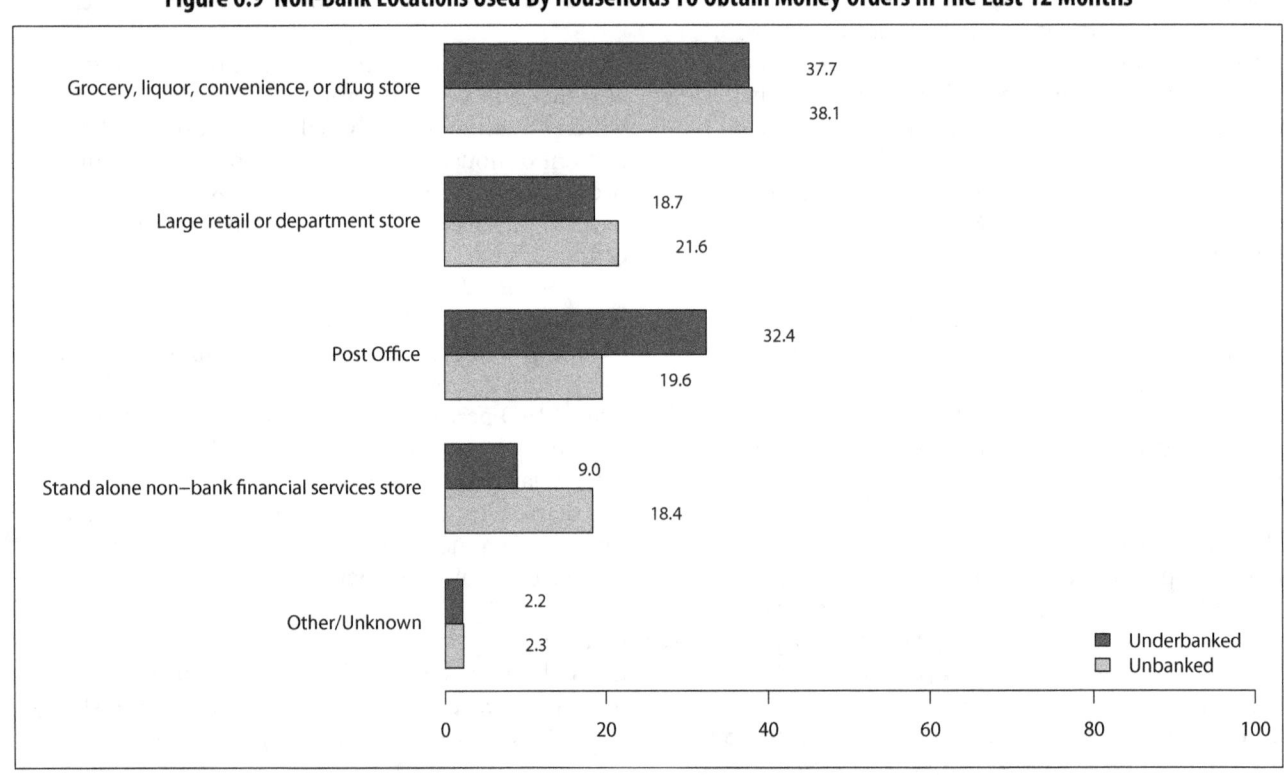

Figure 6.10 Non-Bank Locations Used By Households To Send Remittances In The Last 12 Months

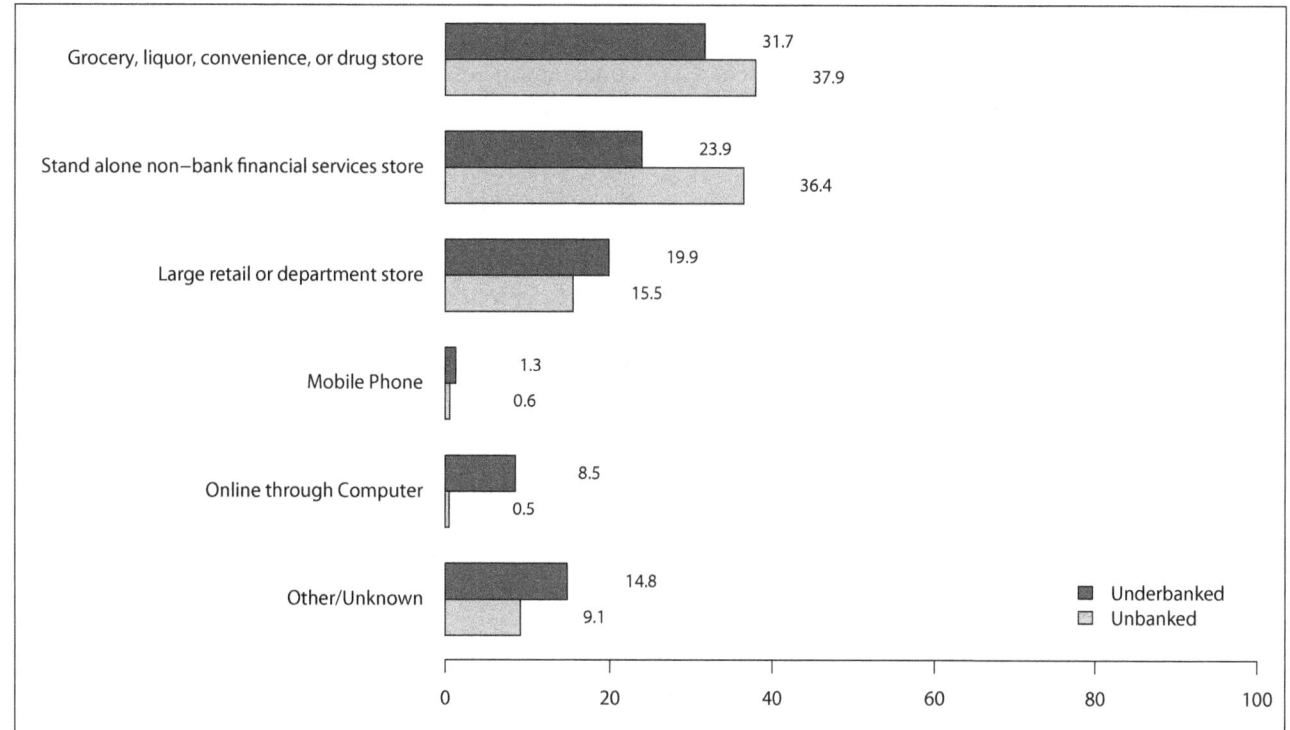

unbanked households that used non-bank check cashing most commonly went to standalone AFS providers, compared to 20.6 percent of underbanked check cashing users. In addition, 36.4 percent of unbanked households that used non-bank remittances did so most commonly at a standalone AFS store, compared to 23.9 percent of underbanked remittance users. The shares of unbanked and underbanked households that used non-bank money orders who most commonly obtained money orders at a standalone AFS store were 18.4 percent and 9.0 percent, respectively.

Underbanked users were more likely to use other locations to obtain AFS. For instance, almost one third (32.4 percent) of underbanked money order users most commonly obtained their money orders from the post office, compared to 19.6 percent of unbanked households that used money orders. Also, almost 10 percent (9.8 percent) of underbanked remittance users used non-bank remittance services online or over their mobile phone most commonly, but only 1.1 percent of unbanked remittance users did so.

The survey did not ask detailed questions about locations from which households obtained most of the credit AFS that they used. However, the survey did question households that had used payday loans about their use of online lending, and found that 15.5 percent of households that used payday loans most commonly obtained them online.

7. Access to Mobile Phones and the Internet

During the past few years, financial institutions, non-bank prepaid card issuers, and AFS providers have placed more emphasis on interacting with customers through the Internet and mobile phones, especially smartphones. Customers must have access to the Internet and to mobile phones to take advantage of these new communication channels. Therefore, the 2013 survey included new questions about household access to mobile phones and the Internet.

Access to Mobile Phones and Smartphones

Table 7.1 Access To Mobile Phones And Smartphones By Banking Status

For all households, column percent

Characteristics	All	Unbanked	Banked: Underbanked	Banked: Fully Banked	Banked: Underbanked Status Unknown
Number of Households (1000s)	123,750	9,582	24,757	82,892	6,519
Percent of Households	100	100	100	100	100
Mobile Phone (Percent)					
Has mobile phone	82.7	68.1	90.5	86.8	22.0
Does not have mobile phone	12.4	25.5	8.5	12.7	3.9
Unknown	4.9	6.4	1.0	0.5	74.2
Smartphone (Percent)					
Smartphone	55.7	33.1	64.5	59.0	13.6
Non-Smartphone	26.5	34.4	25.5	27.5	6.1
No mobile phone	12.4	25.5	8.5	12.7	3.9
Unknown	5.4	6.9	1.5	0.9	76.5

The vast majority of households (82.7 percent) had access to a mobile phone, of which two thirds (67.3 percent of all mobile phones or 55.7 percent overall) were smartphones.[1] Relative to fully banked households, underbanked households were somewhat more likely to have access to a mobile phone (90.5 percent vs. 86.8 percent) or smartphone (64.5 percent vs. 59.0

percent). In contrast, unbanked households were considerably less likely to have access to either a mobile phone (68.1 percent) or a smartphone (33.1 percent). In particular, households that had never been banked had the lowest rates of access to both mobile phones (61.1 percent) and smartphones (26.0 percent).

Access to mobile phones increased with income and education. For example, about 70 percent (71.9 percent) of households with income below $30,000 had access to a mobile phone, compared to 91.6 percent of households with income of at least $75,000. Similarly, two-thirds (67.0 percent) of households without a high school degree had access to a mobile phone compared to 89.5 percent of households with a college degree (see Appendix Table E-2).

The disparity in access by income or education was even more pronounced in the case of access to smartphones. Close to 35 percent (34.8 percent) of those with income below $30,000 have access to a smartphone, compared with almost 80 percent (77.7 percent) of those with income above $75,000 (see Appendix Table E-3).

Access to mobile phones and smartphones also differed by age. Households age 65 or older had considerably lower rates of access to mobile phones (67.3 percent) than their younger counterparts. For example, mobile phone access rates were 83.5 percent for households age 55 to 64 and ranged between 86.6 percent and 89.9 percent for households younger than age 55 (see Appendix Table E-2). The same held true for access to smartphones. Fewer than 1 in 4 households age 65 and older (23.2 percent) had access to smartphones compared with 48.7 percent for households age 55 to 64 and 62.8 percent for households age 45 to 54. Smartphone access rates for households younger than age 45 were considerably higher and ranged from 72.1 percent to 76.5 percent (see Appendix Table E-3).

Internet Access

Three out of four households (75.7 percent) had regular access to the Internet, either at home or outside of the home at locations such as school, work, or the public library. Internet access among underbanked (81.9 percent) and fully banked households

---

[1] The 2013 survey asked households whether they owned or had regular access to a mobile phone. Ownership or regular access to a mobile phone is measured at the household level. The householder might or might not have been a mobile phone user even if the household reported owning or having regular access to a mobile phone. For the purposes of this analysis, the term mobile phone user refers to a household that owned or had regular access to a mobile phone.

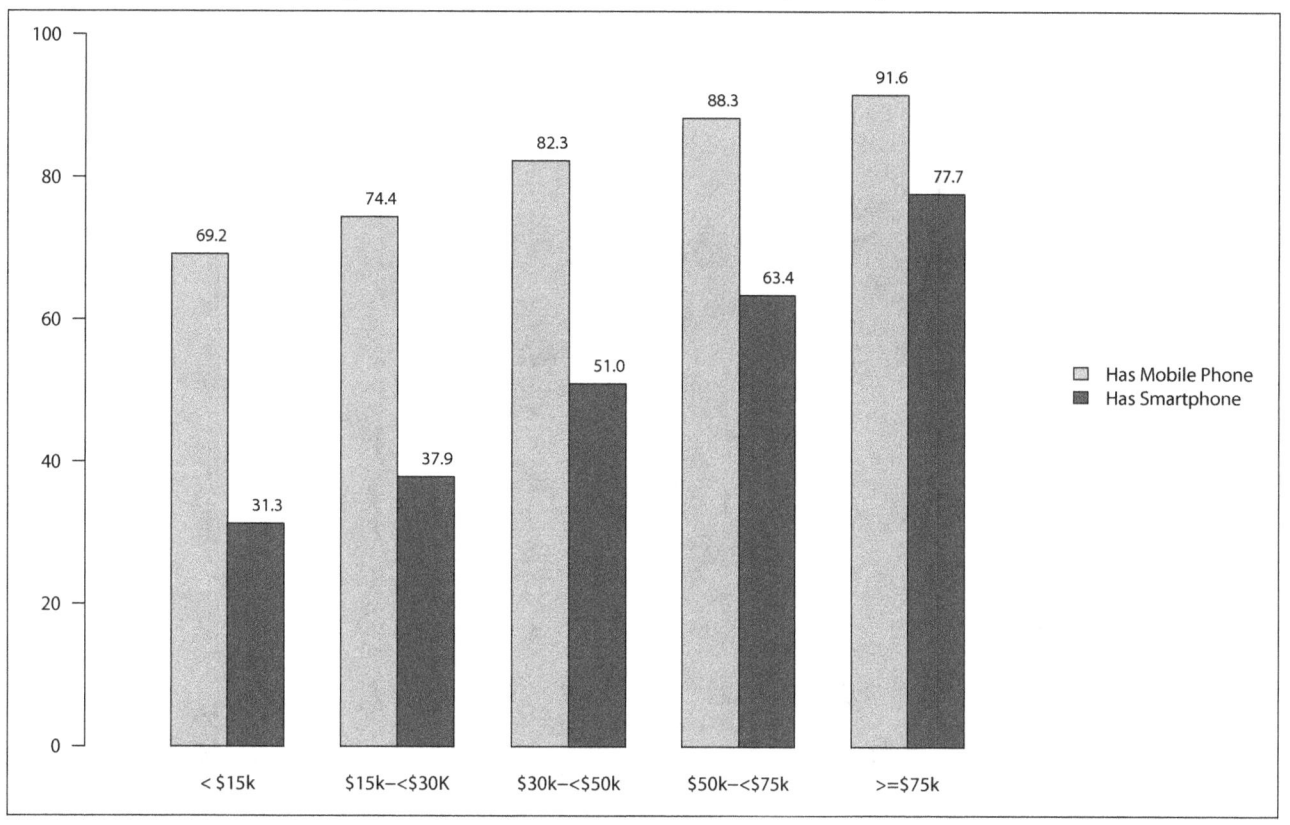

Figure 7.1 Access To Mobile Phones And Smartphones By Income

- Has Mobile Phone
- Has Smartphone

< $15k: 69.2, 31.3
$15k–<$30K: 74.4, 37.9
$30k–<$50k: 82.3, 51.0
$50k–<$75k: 88.3, 63.4
>=$75k: 91.6, 77.7

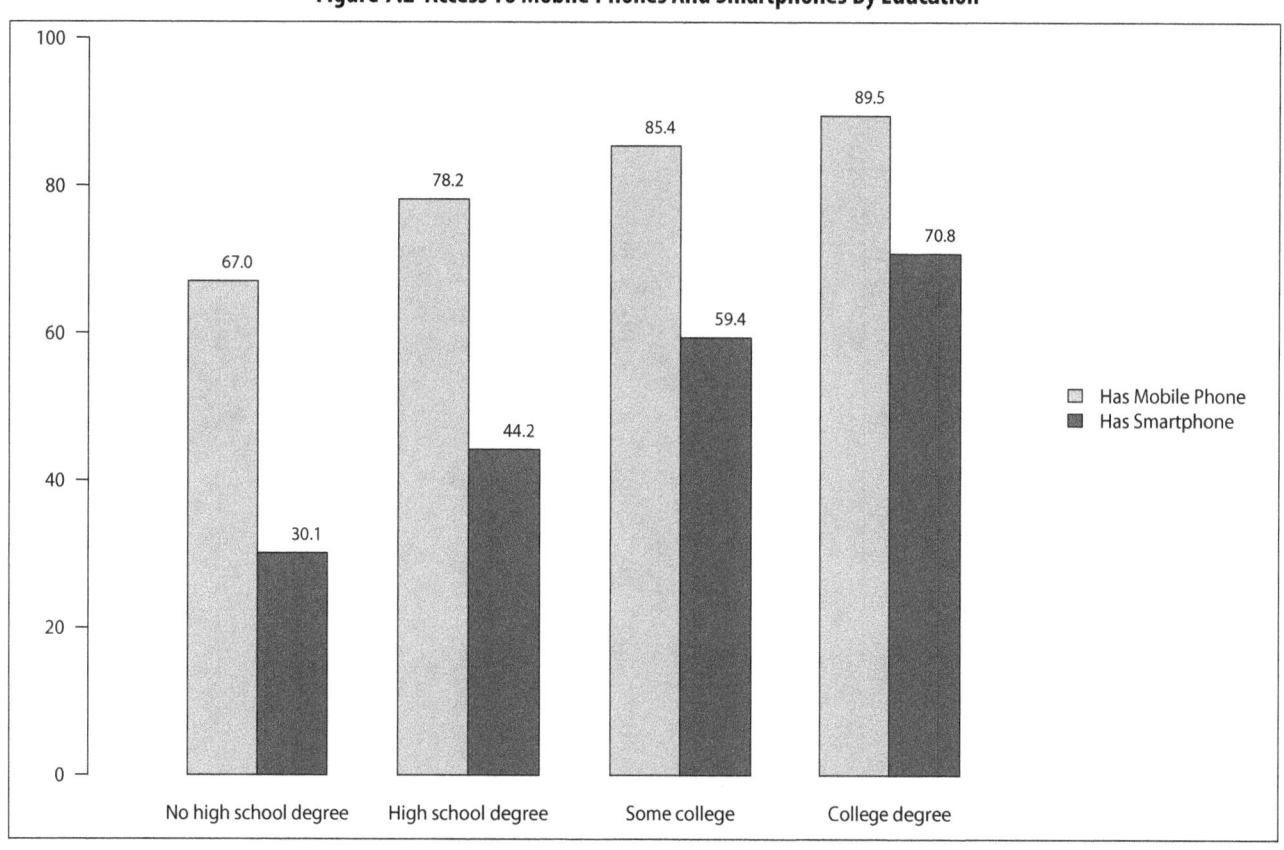

Figure 7.2 Access To Mobile Phones And Smartphones By Education

- Has Mobile Phone
- Has Smartphone

No high school degree: 67.0, 30.1
High school degree: 78.2, 44.2
Some college: 85.4, 59.4
College degree: 89.5, 70.8

Figure 7.3 Access To Mobile Phones And Smartphones By Age

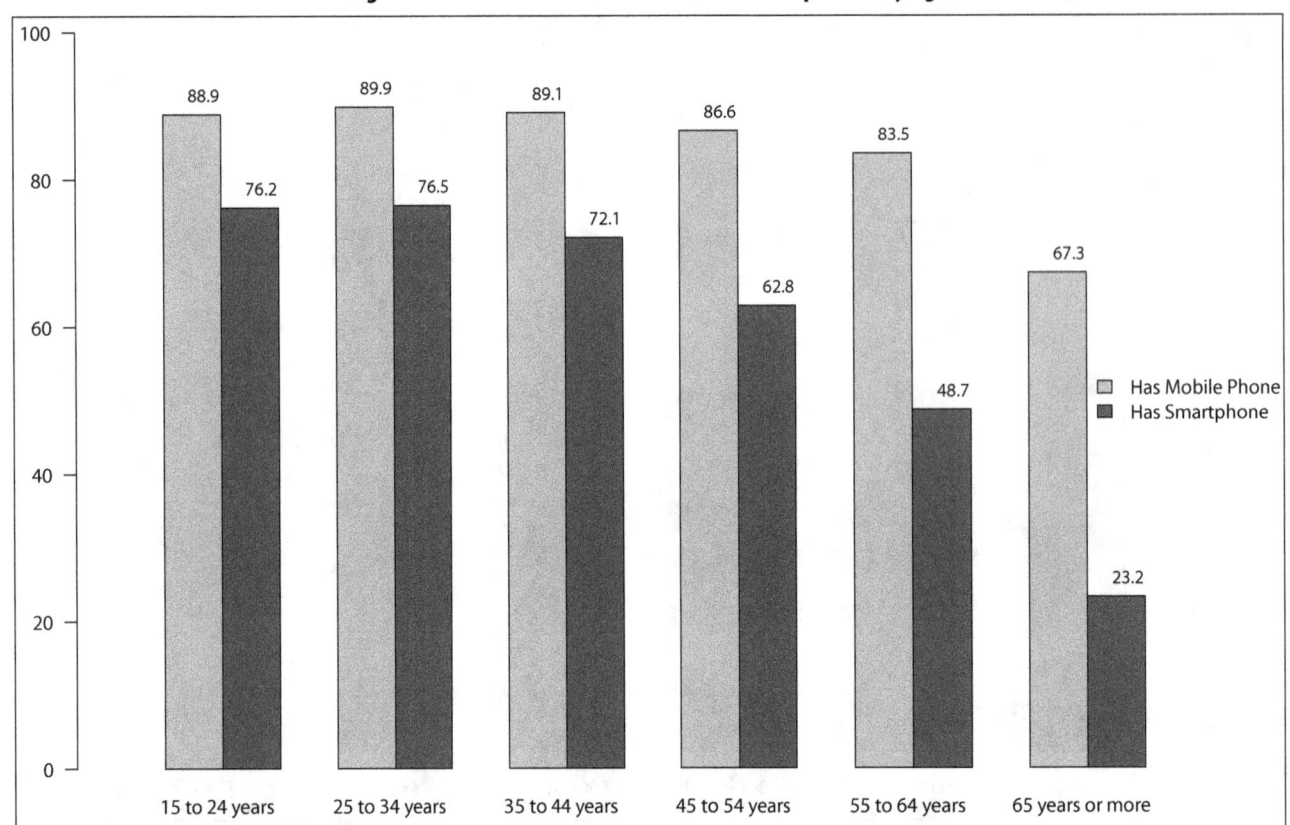

(82.0 percent) were similarly widespread, but unbanked households were considerably less likely to have Internet access (43.0 percent).

Table 7.2 Internet Access By Banking Status

For all households, column percent

Characteristics	All	Unbanked	Banked: Underbanked	Banked: Fully Banked	Banked: Underbanked Status Unknown
Number of Households (1000s)	123,750	9,582	24,757	82,892	6,519
Percent of Households	100	100	100	100	100
Internet Access (Percent)					
Has access	75.7	43.0	81.9	82.0	19.8
Does not have access	19.3	50.2	17.0	17.5	5.1
Unknown	5.0	6.8	1.1	0.5	75.1

Among unbanked households, those that had never been banked had the lowest rate of Internet access (33.3 percent). This group also had the lowest rates of access to mobile phones (61.1 percent) and smartphones (26.0 percent). Previously banked households that had been unbanked for more than 12 months also had lower rates of Internet access (52.2 percent) compared with recently unbanked households (66.6 percent).

Relative to Internet access for White non-Black non-Hispanic households (79.1 percent), significantly lower proportions of black (65.3 percent) and Hispanic (66.4 percent) households had Internet access. Access to the Internet also increased sharply with income and educational attainment (see Appendix Table E-4).

8. Banking Methods

Knowing how households interact with their financial institutions can help inform discussions about how best to serve different groups of consumers. This information can also help illuminate potential effects of bank decisions such as opening or closing branches or providing access to different banking methods (for example, mobile banking) on bringing households into, and keeping them in, the mainstream financial system.

To better understand how banked households interact with their banks, the 2013 survey asked these households whether they had used any of the following in the past 12 months: bank tellers, ATMs/kiosks, telephone banking, online banking, mobile banking, or another banking method.[1] The survey also asked banked households to identify the most common method used, which we refer to in this report as the household's primary or main banking method.

One percent of banked households reported not having accessed their accounts in the last 12 months and another 3.8 percent did not report whether they had accessed their accounts in the same period. All estimates reported in this section are for banked households that reported having accessed their accounts at least once in the last 12 months (95.2 percent of all banked households).

Most banked households used multiple methods to access their bank accounts in the last 12 months. Seven out of ten (71.1 percent) used at least two methods and almost half (47.9 percent) used three or more of these methods.

Figure 8.1 Methods Used To Access Bank Accounts In Last 12 Months

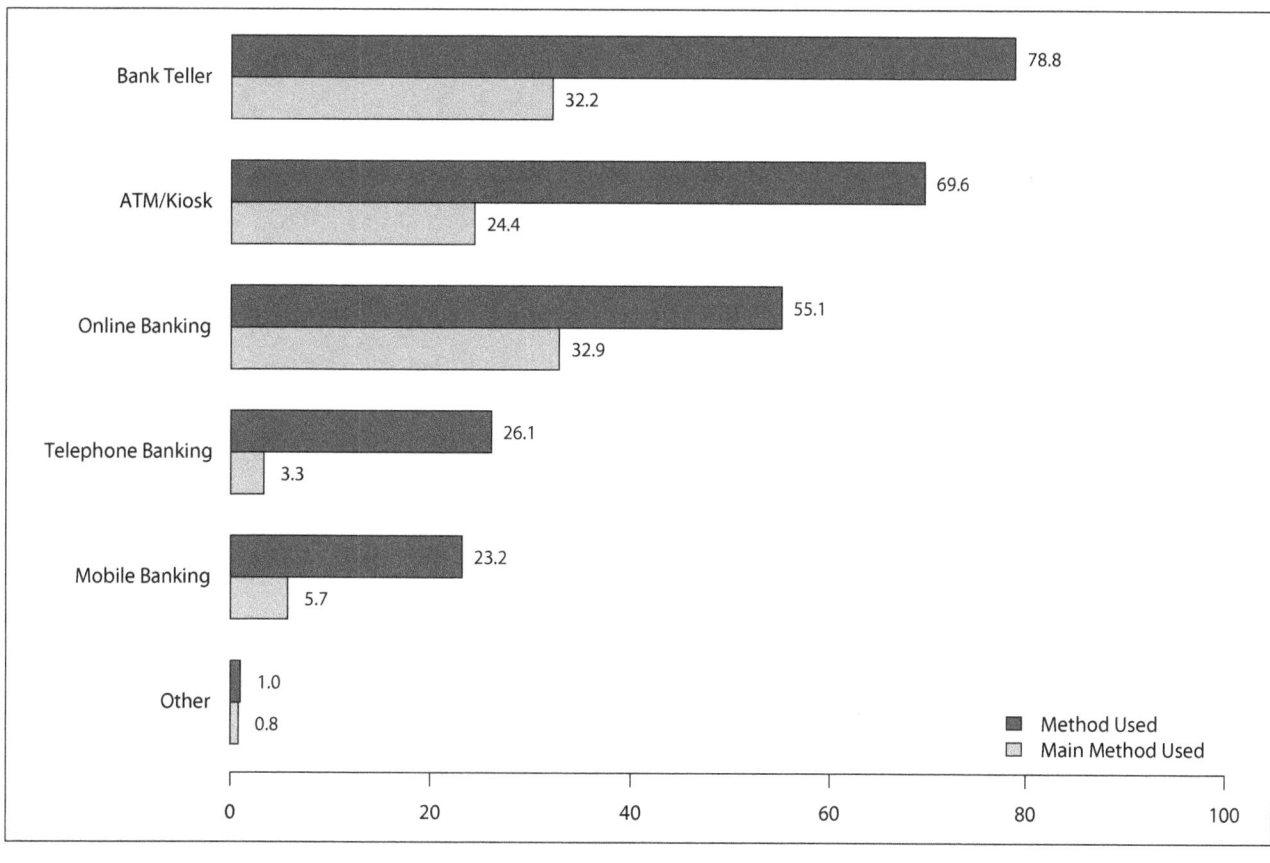

---

[1] Telephone banking was defined as using phone calls or automated voice or touch tone calls to access a bank account. Online banking was defined as accessing a bank account using a desktop or laptop computer, or a tablet such as an iPad. Mobile banking was defined as using text messages, mobile apps, or using a mobile phone's Internet browser or email to access a bank account.

Figure 8.2 All Methods Used To Access Bank Accounts In Last 12 Months By Banking Status

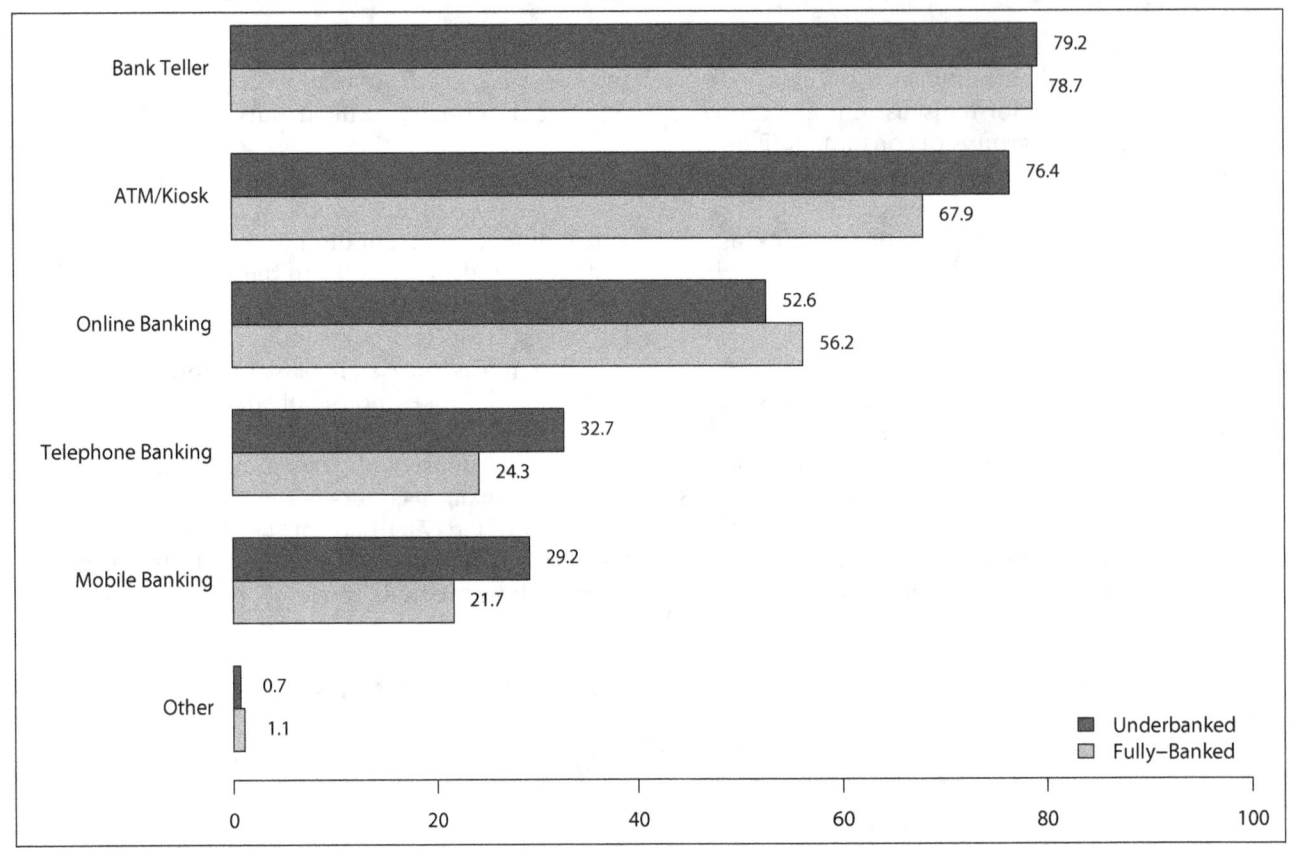

Figure 8.3 Primary Method Used To Access Bank Accounts In Last 12 Months By Banking Status

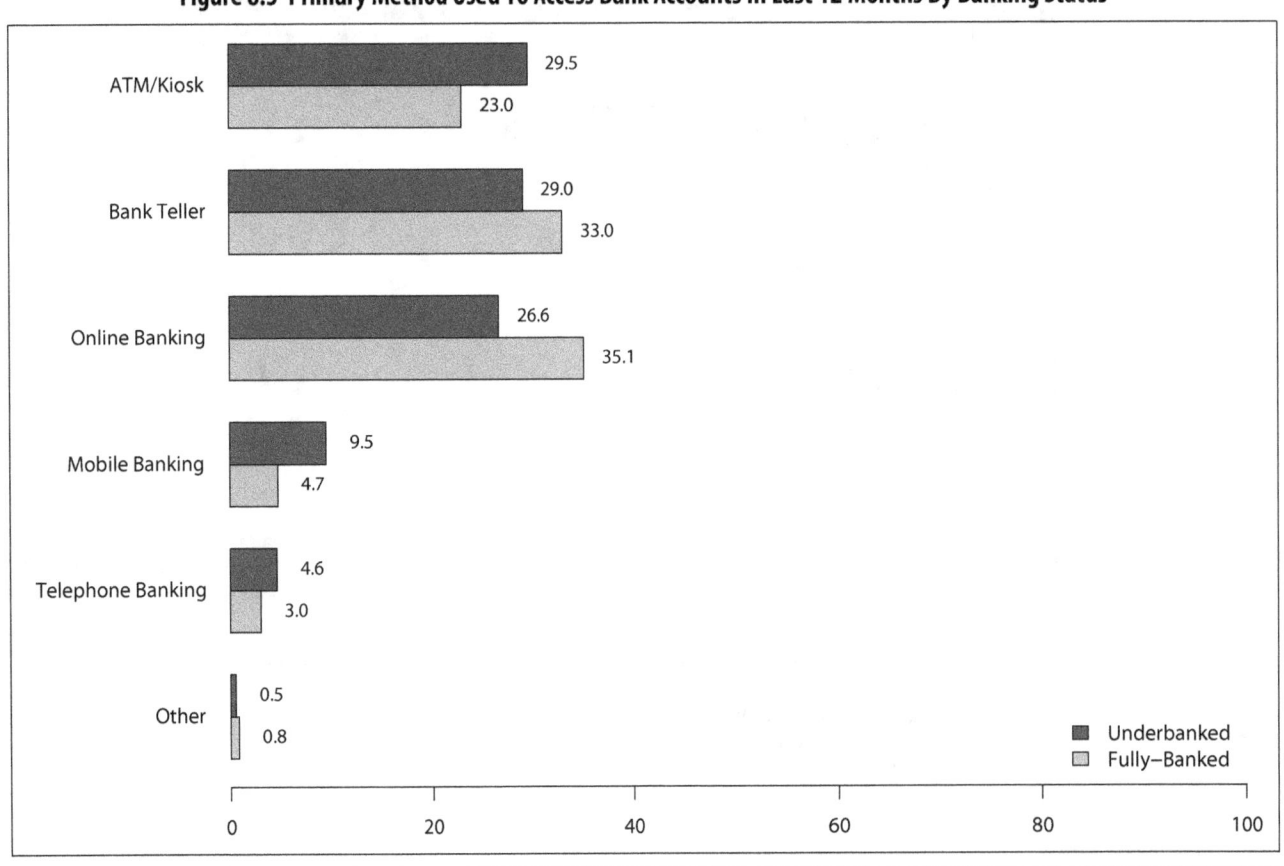

Table 8.1 Main Banking Method By Whether Household Had Internet Access, Mobile Phone Access Or Direct Deposit

For all banked households that accessed their account in the last 12 months, column percent

	All	Has Internet Access	No Internet Access	Has Mobile Phone Access	No Mobile Phone Access	Has Direct Deposit	No Direct Deposit
Number of Households (1000s)	108,295	89,578	19,048	95,811	12,850	91,696	19,071
Percent of Households	100	100	100	100	100	100	100
Main Banking Method (Percent)							
Bank Teller	32.2	25.8	63.0	28.5	59.8	28.7	48.7
ATM/Kiosk	24.4	24.5	24.2	24.8	22.0	24.5	23.8
Telephone Banking	3.3	3.2	4.1	3.3	3.6	3.5	2.5
Online Banking	32.9	38.9	4.7	35.9	11.2	35.8	19.3
Mobile Banking	5.7	6.7	1.3	6.5	0.4	6.0	4.6
Other	0.8	0.5	2.4	0.5	2.7	0.8	0.5
Unknown	0.7	0.6	0.3	0.6	0.3	0.7	0.6

Use of Banking Methods by Banking Status

Among banked households that accessed their accounts in the last 12 months, the vast majority used bank tellers (78.8 percent) or ATMs/kiosks (69.6 percent), while more than half used online banking (55.1 percent) and almost a quarter (23.2 percent) used mobile banking.[2]

Bank tellers and online banking were the primary methods used by the largest share of households. Equal shares of banked households (almost a third each) reported using online banking and bank tellers as their most common banking method in the last 12 months. Almost a quarter of banked households said they most commonly used ATMs/kiosks and 5.7 percent said they primarily used mobile banking.

Regardless of whether the household was fully banked or underbanked, bank tellers, ATMs/kiosks, and online banking were the top three primary methods used, although their order and the relative shares of households that used each method differed slightly by banking status. Underbanked households were less likely to use online banking as their main banking method (26.6 percent) compared with fully banked households (35.1 percent). Conversely, underbanked households were more likely to use mobile banking as their main banking method (9.5 percent) compared with fully banked households (4.7 percent).

Primary Banking Method and Direct Deposit, Internet Access and Mobile Phone Access

Higher proportions of households without direct deposit, Internet access or mobile phone access used bank tellers as their primary method of accessing their accounts in the last 12 months. Households without direct deposit, Internet access or mobile phone access were also less likely to use online banking as their primary method (see Table 8.1).

Use of Banking Methods by Household Characteristics

Income and Education

Banked households with lower income or educational attainment were considerably more likely than higher-income or more educated households to bank primarily through bank tellers and were less likely to bank primarily online. While this result is consistent with the lower rates of Interent access among lower-income and less educated households, they were less likely to use online banking and more likely to use bank tellers even after taking into account their lower rates of Internet access. For example, households with incomes of less than $30,000 were more than twice as likely to primarily use bank tellers than online banking. In contrast, households with incomes between $50,000 and $75,000 and incomes of at least $75,000 were much more likely (a third to more than two times more likely) to mainly use online banking than bank tellers (see Appendix Table F-2).

---

[2] Estimates do not reflect the frequency of use, only whether households used a particular access method at least once in the last 12 months.

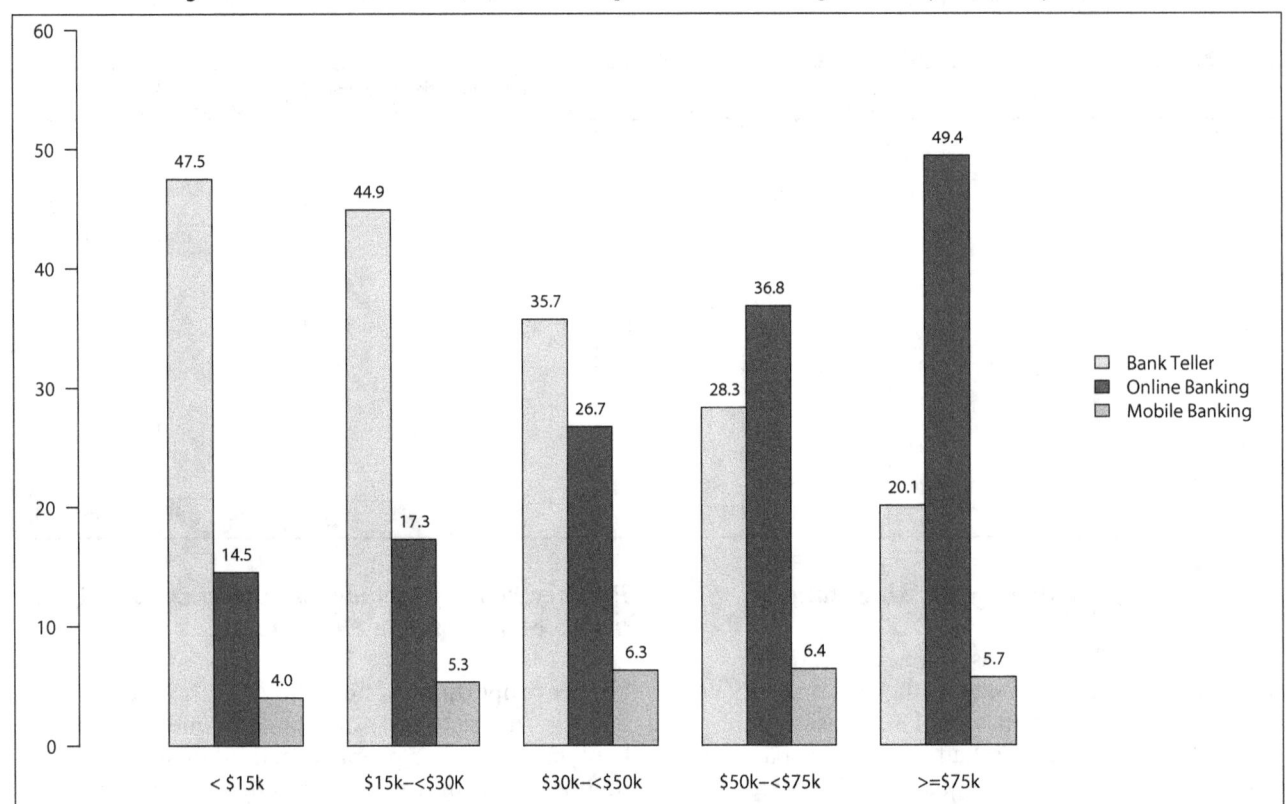

Figure 8.4 Use of Bank Tellers, Online Banking And Mobile Banking As Primary Method By Income

Similarly, less than 10 percent (8.8 percent) of households without a high school degree banked primarily online, compared to close to half (48.0 percent) of households with college degrees. Over half (55.6 percent) of the households without a high school degree and more than two out of five (41.8 percent) households with a high school degree used bank tellers as their main banking method, relative to one in five (21.0 percent) households with a college degree (see Appendix Table F-2).

Age

Differences in banking methods by age were also quite distinct. Considerably higher proportions of households age 45 and above most commonly used a bank teller compared to households under age 45. For example, more than half of households age 65 and above (54.6 percent) primarily used bank tellers, compared with 36.1 percent of households age 55 to 64 and 26.7 percent of households age 45 to 54. For households age 44 and below, the share that primarily used bank tellers ranged from 17.0 percent to 21.1 percent.

The opposite was true for mobile banking, which was considerably more prevalent among younger households. While one in five (20.3 percent) households

under age 25 primarily used mobile banking, less than 10 percent of households age 35 and above did so.

The use of online banking also decreased with householder age, with the exception of the youngest households (under age 24). These households had the second lowest rate (27.8 percent) and the oldest households (age 65 and above) had the lowest rate (17.8 percent) of using online banking as their primary banking method. See Appendix Table F-2 for more detail on differences in banking methods by age.

Race and Ethnicity

Black (21.4 percent) and Hispanic (23.0 percent) households were significantly less likely to use online banking as their primary method for accessing accounts compared with Non-Black Non-Hispanic White households (35.8 percent). While this is consistent with their lower rates of Internet access, they were less likely to use online banking as their primary method even after taking into account their lower rates of Internet access.

Black (31.6 percent) and Hispanic (29.9 percent) households were also more likely to use ATMs/kiosks

Figure 8.5 Use Of Bank Tellers, Online Banking And Mobile Banking As Primary Method By Education

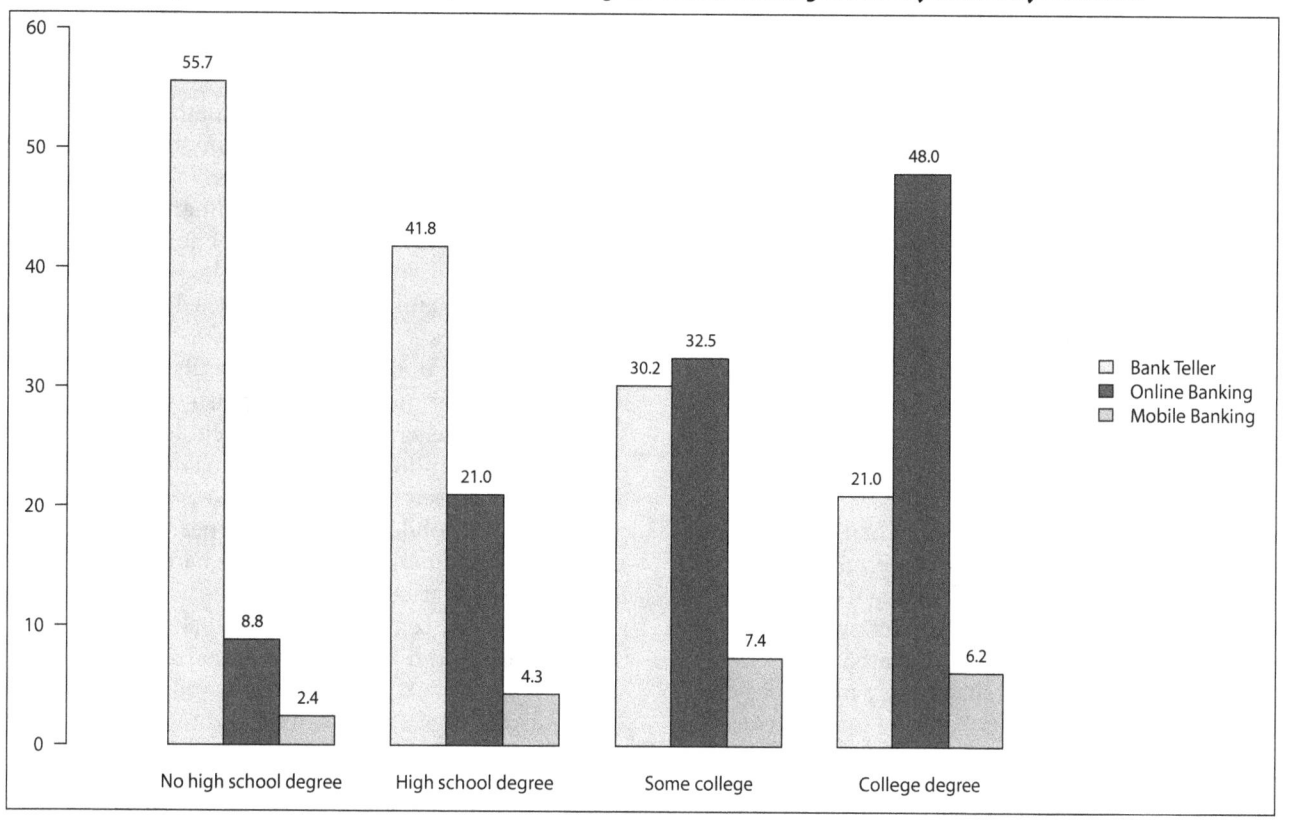

Figure 8.6 Use Of Bank Tellers, Online Banking And Mobile Banking As Primary Method by Age

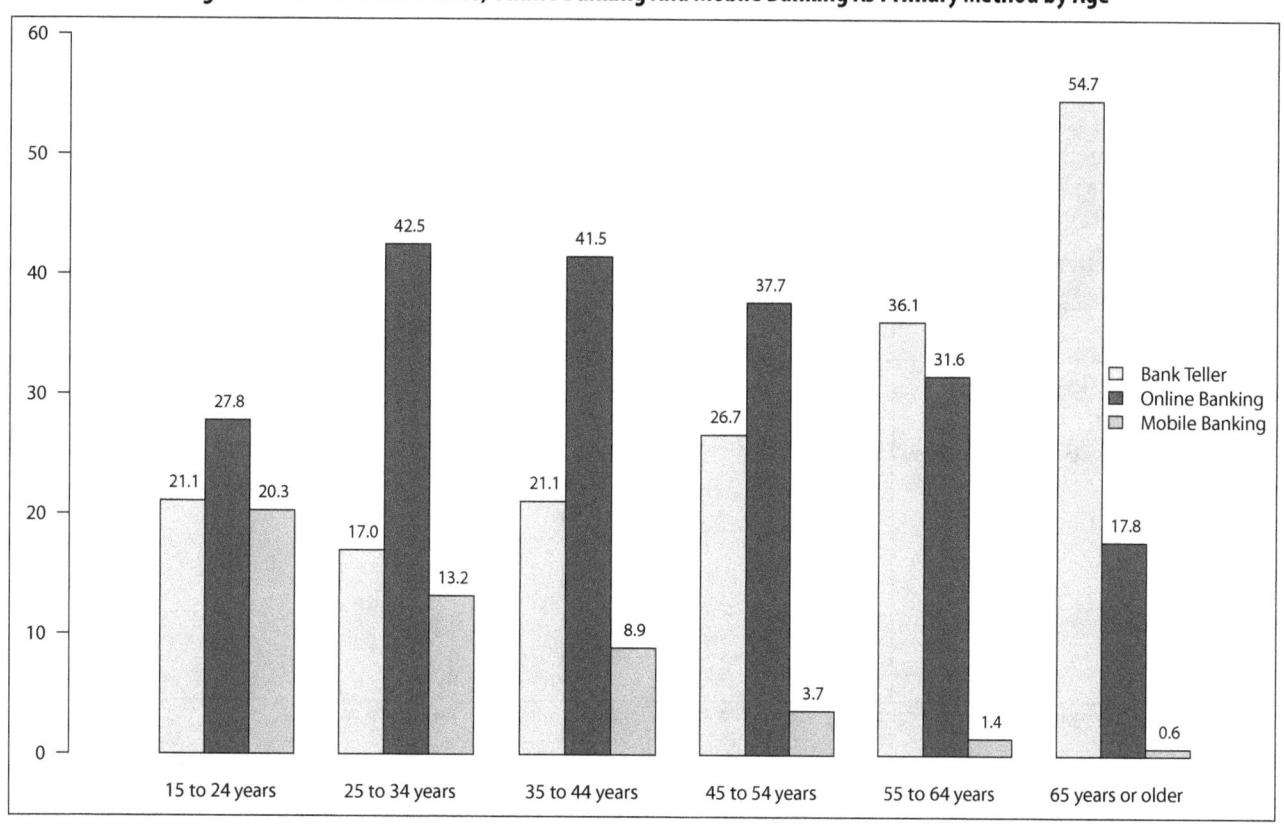

as their primary method for accessing their accounts, compared to 22.5 percent of Non-Black Non-Hispanic White households.

Use of A Single Banking Method

As noted previously, 71.1 percent of banked households used more than one banking method to access their account in the last 12 months. However, three in ten households (28.8 percent) used only one method. Among households that used only one method to access their account, the majority (60.7 percent) used a bank teller, one in five (19.8 percent) used only an ATM and 13.2 percent used only online banking.

The use of bank tellers as the only banking channel was heavily concentrated among certain demographic groups. Households that exclusively used bank tellers were more likely to be age 65 and above, had incomes under $30,000, and were less educated. Households in rural areas were also considerably more likely to use tellers as their primary banking method (see Appendix Table F-3).

Use of Multiple Banking Methods

The number of banking methods used also varied depending on the household's primary banking method. Most households that primarily used bank tellers to access their accounts used them as the only banking method (54.2 percent) or along with one other banking method (25.0 percent). In contrast, most households that mainly banked online used 2 additional banking methods (median number of

banking methods was 3). Households that primarily used mobile banking used 3 additional methods (median number of banking methods used was 4).

Examining the additional banking methods used in conjunction with the primary method, the survey shows that ATMs were the most likely secondary method used by households that primarily banked via teller (37.2 percent). The majority of households that primarily banked online or via mobile banking used a variety of other banking methods (see Table 8.3).

More than three out of four households that primarily used online or mobile banking also used ATMs/kiosks or bank tellers. Among households that primarily used online banking, a considerable share (78.1 percent) used ATMs/kiosks, bank tellers (71.9 percent), and mobile banking (35.0 percent). Only 11.6 percent exclusively used online banking. Among households that used mobile banking as their primary method, 84.6 percent used ATMs/kiosks, 79.5 percent banked online, and 71.1 percent used bank tellers. Only 7.5 percent exclusively used mobile banking. These results suggest that online and mobile banking are still a complement to more traditional banking methods.

Results were generally similar regardless of banking status: underbanked households were slightly more likely to use additional methods than fully banked households. The number of banking methods used increased sharply with income and educational attainment.[3] Results by age indicated a stark contrast between households age 65 or older relative to younger households. Almost half (47.7 percent) of the households age 65 and older exclusively used one banking method, a markedly higher proportion than

Table 8.2 Number Of Banking Methods Used By Primary Method

For all banked households that accessed their account in the last 12 months, column percent

	All	Bank Teller	ATM/Kiosk	Telephone Banking	Online Banking	Mobile Banking	Other	Unknown
Number of Households (1000s)	108,295	34,897	26,398	3,591	35,600	6,192	846	773
Percent of Households	100	100	100	100	100	100	100	100
Number of Banking Methods Used (Percent)								
1 Method	28.8	54.2	23.4	22.9	11.6	7.5	81.5	-
2 Methods	23.2	25.0	34.9	17.9	16.1	7.8	9.7	39.6
3 Methods	22.5	12.7	22.9	28.3	32.6	18.0	2.6	25.4
4 to 6 Methods	25.4	8.2	18.8	30.9	39.7	66.7	6.1	35.0
Mean	2.5	1.8	2.4	2.8	3.1	3.7	1.4	3.0
Median	2.0	1.0	2.0	3.0	3.0	4.0	1.0	3.0

-= For this table cell, the estimated proportion would round to zero. The population proportion, however, is likely to be slightly greater than zero.

---

[3] Even when controlling for the primary method of use, income and education appear to have an effect on the number of banking methods households used to access their bank account.

Table 8.3 All Banking Methods Used By Main Banking Method

For all banked households that accessed their account in the last 12 months, column percent

	All	Bank Teller	ATM/Kiosk	Telephone Banking	Online Banking	Mobile Banking	Other	Unknown
Number of Households (1000s)	108,295	34,897	26,398	3,591	35,600	6,192	846	773
Percent of Households	100	100	100	100	100	100	100	100
All Methods								
Bank Teller (Percent)								
Yes	78.8	100.0	65.7	64.4	71.9	71.1	13.2	87.8
No	21.2	-	34.3	35.6	28.1	28.9	86.8	12.2
ATM/Kiosk (Percent)								
Yes	69.6	37.2	100.0	61.1	78.1	84.6	9.7	90.1
No	30.4	62.8	-	38.9	21.9	15.4	90.3	9.9
Telephone Banking (Percent)								
Yes	26.1	14.5	24.0	100.0	29.6	38.7	6.8	37.8
No	73.9	85.5	76.0	-	70.4	61.3	93.2	62.2
Online Banking (Percent)								
Yes	55.1	20.0	39.2	36.0	100.0	79.5	6.0	63.0
No	44.9	80.0	60.8	64.0	-	20.5	94.0	37.0
Mobile Banking (Percent)								
Yes	23.2	5.4	14.6	16.2	35.0	100.0	1.3	28.0
No	76.8	94.6	85.4	83.8	65.0	-	98.7	72.0
Other (Percent)								
Yes	1.0	0.2	0.2	0.3	0.4	0.2	100.0	0.7
No	99.0	99.8	99.8	99.7	99.6	99.8	-	99.3

-= For this table cell, the estimated proportion would round to zero. The population proportion, however, is likely to be slightly greater than zero.

that prevailing among younger households. For example, less than a quarter (22.8 percent) of households below age 55 used one banking method.

Use of Mobile Banking

Mobile banking is an emerging banking method that has raised the interest of industry and policy stakeholders as a potential tool for economic inclusion. To gain insight into this potential and understand how consumers are using this new delivery channel, the 2013 survey included additional questions on access to mobile technology, including use of the Internet and mobile phones, and the types of activities that consumers perform via mobile banking. Survey results show a higher incidence of mobile banking among underbanked consumers relative to the fully banked. Underbanked consumers also were more likely to use mobile as their primary banking method. If mobile banking adoption continues to follow this pattern, clear opportunities may emerge to use mobile to more fully-financially engage underbanked consumers.

Overall, 23.2 percent of banked households that accessed their account in the past 12 months used mobile banking. Mobile banking usage among households with access to smartphones was even higher (36.2 percent).

A greater share of underbanked households (29.2 percent) used mobile banking than fully banked households (21.7 percent) when smartphone access was not taken into account. Underbanked households with access to smartphones (42.0 percent) were also more likely to use mobile banking compared with fully banked households with access to smartphones (34.0 percent).

Main Banking Method Among Households That Used Mobile Banking

As mobile banking draws more consumers, it is useful to see how households that use this emerging channel interact with their financial institutions. Consistent with expectations, the large majority of households that used mobile banking (49.5 percent) primarily banked online, and one-quarter (24.6 percent) used mobile banking as their main banking method. In fact, the share of mobile banking users that used tellers as their main banking method (7.4 percent) was considerably lower than that of non-mobile banking users (39.7 percent).

Table 8.4 Primary Banking Method Used By Households That Did And Did Not Use Mobile Banking

For all banked households that accessed their account in the last 12 months, column percent

	All	Used Mobile Banking (Percent)	Did Not Use Mobile Banking (Percent)
Number of Households (1000s)	108,295	25,165	83,130
Percent of Households	100	100	100
Primary Banking Method (Percent)			
Bank Teller	32.2	7.4	39.7
ATM/Kiosk	24.4	15.3	27.1
Telephone Banking	3.3	2.3	3.6
Online Banking	32.9	49.5	27.9
Mobile Banking	5.7	24.6	-
Other	0.8	-	1.0
Unknown	0.7	0.9	0.7

-= For this table cell, the estimated proportion would round to zero. The population proportion, however, is likely to be slightly greater than zero.

Among mobile banking users, the use of online and mobile banking technology differed by banking status. Underbanked mobile banking users were considerably less likely (38.1 percent) than fully banked mobile banking users (54.2 percent) to use online banking as their main banking method. In contrast, underbanked households that used mobile banking were more likely (32.4 percent) to rely on it as their primary method than fully banked households that used mobile banking (21.6 percent).

Types of Mobile Banking Activity Among Households That Used Mobile Banking

Monitoring bank account balances and recent transactions were the most common mobile banking activities, used by 86.0 percent of all mobile banking users. Only a quarter (25.5 percent) of households that used mobile banking deposited a check via mobile.

Results by banking status were very similar. The most noticeable difference is that underbanked households were somewhat more likely (51.5 percent) to receive text message alerts than fully banked households (44.6 percent).

Although the emergence of online and mobile banking facilitates the electronic delivery of banking services, adoption rates vary widely across subgroups. For most demographic segments, even those who bank primarily online or via mobile, bank tellers continue to be an important banking method. It is important to continue tracking these trends and the disparities in adoption. In particular, it is valuable to understand how changes in delivery channels can create opportunities to serve certain segments of the underserved population. However, changes in delivery methods can create additional challenges to serving those who heavily rely on more traditional channels if they are not as widely offered. Identifying the specific segments affected can be valuable in thinking about banking delivery strategies and balancing the availability of banking channels, including opportunities to effectively help certain segments transition.

Figure 8.7 Primary Banking Method Used By Mobile Banking Users By Banking Status

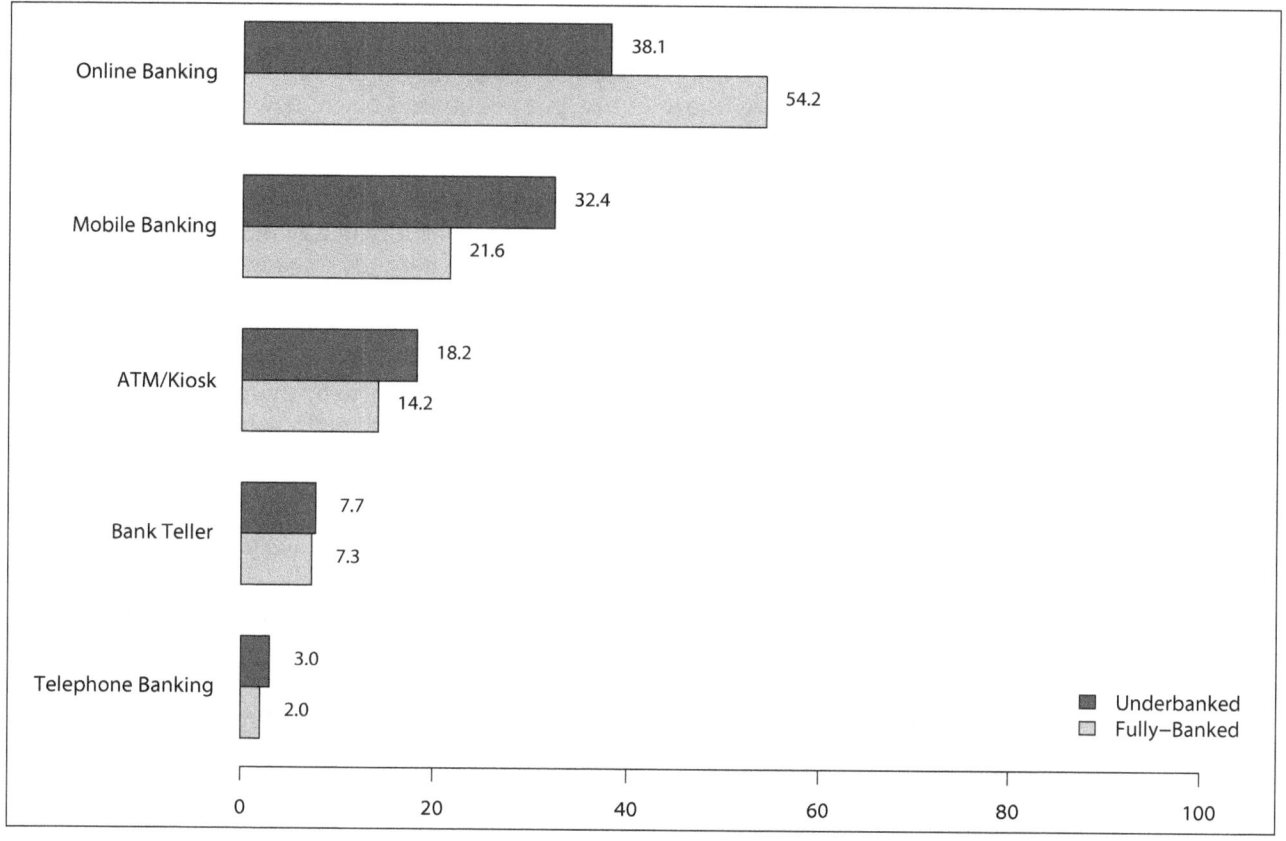

Figure 8.8 Types Of Mobile Banking Activity By Banking Status

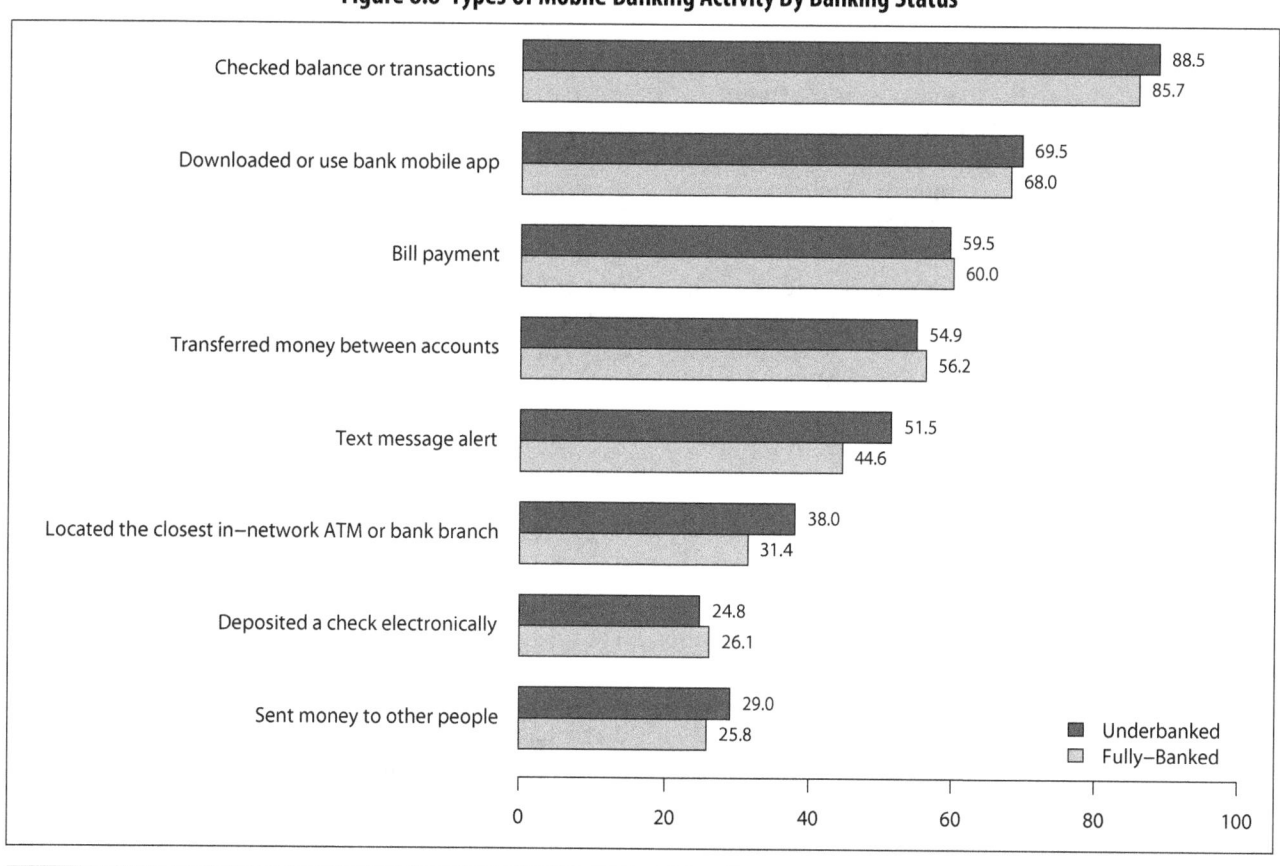

9. Implications and Conclusion

The survey results presented in this report show a 0.5 percentage point drop in the unbanked rate over the two-year period between June 2011 and June 2013. This change is, in part, a function of those entering and exiting the banking system. In the 12 months prior to the survey, the proportion of households that established a banking relationship (1.6 percent) was larger than the proportion that exited the banking system (0.7 percent). Future changes in the unbanked rate will continue to be influenced by the rate at which new households enter the banking system and the sustainability of established banking relationships. The results also demonstrated significant growth in the use of prepaid debit cards, particularly among unbanked households, who used them to facilitate common financial transactions. Finally, the survey highlighted both the potential of mobile financial services to increase convenience for underserved consumers and the continued importance of bank branches and other banking channels. These results suggest implications for policymakers, financial institutions and other stakeholders who are working to improve access to mainstream financial services, better retain customers in the banking system, and consider opportunities presented by mobile technology to provide convenient services.

1. Entrances and exits from the banking system are often associated with changes in employment and income. Interventions designed to help households maintain and renew their banking relationships through economic challenges may reduce unbanked rates over time.

Banking status is dynamic; many households cycle in and out of the banking system. About half of all unbanked households have had a bank account in the past, and many of these report being likely to open another account in the future. Almost one in ten unbanked households became unbanked in the last 12 months and these recently unbanked households are among the most likely to report wanting to open another account in the future.

These findings suggest that economic inclusion efforts should focus both on bringing consumers into the mainstream banking system and on retaining current customers by better engaging and meeting the needs of those at risk of becoming unbanked. In order to do so, it is important to understand the circumstances that lead households to transition in and out of banking, as this can inform efforts to attract or retain these customers.

In many cases, financial life events, such as job loss, significant income loss or a new job, appear to be important reasons why households leave or enter the banking system. Recently unbanked households were relatively more likely to have experienced adverse financial life events such as job loss or significant income loss. Because these results show that adverse financial events appear to be more closely associated with bank account closing decisions than other types of life events, policy makers and industry participants might consider ways to cushion the impact of adverse financial shocks on a household's ability or desire to maintain a bank account. In particular, opportunities may exist for forbearance of fees, flexible product design, or direct interventions. Interventions could include targeted outreach or financial education for recently unemployed households to encourage them to remain in the banking system, for example.

Recently banked households were relatively more likely to report a new job and to report that the new job contributed to the household becoming banked. In addition, the most frequently reported reason that recently banked households cited for opening an account was to receive direct deposits. These findings suggest that opportunities may exist for bringing newly employed consumers into the financial mainstream and helping them successfully maintain their accounts by educating them on the use of bank accounts and personal financial management. Opportunities may also exist to reach out to employers that do not yet offer direct deposit to help them lower costs and help their employees better understand the opportunities offered by the mainstream banking system.

2. Unbanked households are increasingly turning to general purpose reloadable prepaid cards to address their financial transaction needs and are generally obtaining them at non-bank locations. Opportunities may exist to meet these consumers' needs within the banking system.

While the use of prepaid cards has increased among all banking status groups, the growth has been particularly fast among unbanked households. In fact, the proportion of unbanked households that have ever used prepaid cards more than doubled between 2009 and 2013, to more than 27 percent. The vast majority of these unbanked prepaid card users are obtaining their cards from a non-bank location, but are using the cards to perform basic financial transactions that otherwise could be performed using banking services.

Almost half of unbanked households that use prepaid cards, like other unbanked households, are unbanked primarily because they perceive they "do not have enough money to maintain an account or meet a minimum balance" or because they perceive that "bank fees are too high or unpredictable." Although these households may perceive that their financial circumstances prevent them from having a banking relationship, they still have a demonstrated need for financial services to assist them with basic transactions, such as receiving and making payments. In fact, four out of five unbanked prepaid card users use the cards to "pay for everyday purchases or bills" or to "receive payments." Banking products such as a low cost, safe transaction account or a bank prepaid debit card that meets the specifications of the FDIC Safe Accounts Template could help meet the financial transactions needs of these consumers while building banking relationships.

Almost half of unbanked households that use prepaid cards report being likely to open a bank account in the near future. In addition to the demonstrated demand for financial services evidenced by prepaid card customers, the results show that previously banked households are almost two and a half times more likely to use prepaid cards than households that have never been banked. Also, having previous banking experience is associated with a greater inclination to open an account. Consequently, these results suggest that significant opportunities may exist for unbanked prepaid card users to enter or rejoin the banking system.

3. **Mobile banking is a potential tool to encourage economic inclusion but bank branches continue to play an important role for many consumers, including those who are underbanked.**

Mobile technology appears to have promise to help expand economic inclusion based in part on its potential to enhance the convenience of banking transactions. The 2009 and 2011 surveys found that many households use transaction AFS mainly because of convenience. Mobile technology provides consumers with the ability to conveniently conduct transactions and view account balances anytime and anywhere.

For mobile technologies to improve economic inclusion among the underserved, these consumers must have access to mobile phones, particularly smartphones. The 2013 survey shows that mobile phone access is prevalent among banked households, especially among the underbanked. In fact, underbanked households are more likely than fully banked households to own a smartphone and they are more likely than fully banked households to use mobile banking and to use it as their main banking channel. These findings suggest that underbanked consumers are well-positioned to take advantage of mobile banking.

In addition, mobile technologies might also become useful tools for bringing unbanked households into the financial mainstream. While cell phone access is less common among unbanked households than among the underbanked and fully banked, it is still relatively high. More than two-thirds of unbanked households have access to mobile phones, almost half of which are smartphones, while fewer than half of unbanked households have regular Internet access. Innovations such as mobile account opening could play a role in expanding access to banking for the unbanked.

From the supply side, basic mobile banking offerings are becoming ubiquitous, and more comprehensive functionalities are being deployed all the time. However, as discussed in the 2014 FDIC report "Assessing The Economic Inclusion Potential of Mobile Financial Services", mobile banking offerings are not always implemented in ways that facilitate economic inclusion.[1] For example, mobile banking is often designed to work together with online banking. To access mobile banking, users often must have an online-enabled bank account and use online banking. And, sometimes certain mobile banking features, such as mobile banking alerts, need to be set up or changed via an online banking platform. Although underbanked and fully banked households have regular access to the Internet at similar rates, the use of online banking as the main banking method is considerably less prevalent among the underbanked. This suggests that mobile banking's interdependence with online banking could constrain underbanked households' ability to take advantage of the full array of mobile banking functionalities.

Having mobile banking function more completely as a standalone channel would not necessarily diminish

---

[1] See Susan Burhouse, Matthew Homer, Yazmin Osaki, and Michael Bachman, "Assessing the Economic Inclusion Potential of Mobile Financial Services," June 30, 2014, available at https://www.fdic.gov/consumers/community/mobile/Mobile-Financial-Services.pdf.

the importance of other banking methods. On the contrary, other banking channels continue to be widely used and are important for economic inclusion and outreach efforts. In fact, the majority of both fully banked and underbanked households that use mobile banking as their primary channel also use a bank branch. Traditional banking channels, such as branches, provide functions not currently available through online and mobile banking. For example, consumers that need to purchase money orders or cash a check generally need to go to a bank teller. In addition, FDIC pilot studies have found that branch staff play an important role in making underserved consumers aware of products, providing basic financial education, and growing their banking relationships.[2]

As banking technologies continue to evolve, it is important to continue tracking how households access banking services. To this end, policymakers, practitioners and other stakeholders can look for feasible ways to make all mobile banking functionalities more accessible to underserved consumers, while also continuing to evaluate the role that branches play in providing transaction services and assess opportunities to grow banking relationships with underserved consumers through mobile and non-mobile channels.

---

[2] See Rae-Ann Miller, Susan Burhouse, Luke Reynolds and Aileen Sampson, "A Template for Success: The FDIC's Small Dollar Loan Pilot Program," FDIC Quarterly 2010, Volume 4, No. 2 and Sherrie Rhine and Susan Burhouse, "FDIC Model Safe Accounts Pilot: Final Report," April 2012.